# by Josh Azouz

*Buggy Baby* was first performed at The Yard,
London, on 7 March 2018.

# BUGGY BABY
## by Josh Azouz

**Cast**

| | |
|---|---|
| NUR | Hoda Bentaher |
| JADEN | Noof McEwan |
| BABY AYA | Jasmine Jones |
| GUNSHOT-WOUND RABBIT | Tom Clegg |
| BURNT-FUR RABBIT | Abrahim Jarman |

**Creative Team**

| | |
|---|---|
| *Director* | Ned Bennett |
| *Designer* | Max Johns |
| *Lighting Designer* | Jess Bernberg |
| *Composer and Sound Designer* | Giles Thomas |
| *Casting Director* | Sophie Parrott CDG |
| *Production Manager* | Seb Cannings |
| *Stage Manager on the Book* | Edwina Allen |
| *Assistant Stage Manager* | Kate Clement |

The first run of *Buggy Baby* was supported by Arts Council England.

# Cast and Creative Team

### Hoda Bentaher NUR
Theatre includes: *Shakespeare Within the Abbey* (Shakespeare Globe), *Sonnet Walks* (Shakespeare Globe), *The Suit* (Young Vic Theatre), *Sixteen* (The Gate Theatre), *Julius Caesar* (Intermission Theatre), *Verona Road* (Intermission Theatre). Film and television includes: *Casualty* (BBC).

### Jasmine Jones BABY AYA
Theatre includes: *This Child* (Southwark Playhouse), *Arden of Faversham* (RSC), *Phillipa and Will are Now in a Relationship* (Misshapen Theatre), *Gilgamesh* (Cheek by Jowl). Jasmine also works with all-female theatre companies Dangerous Space and Flock Theatre. Film, Television and Radio includes: *50 Ways To Kill Your Lover* (Thumbs Up Productions/Discovery ID), *Diego Story* (Wayne Yip), *Threepenny Dosshouse* (Double Diddy Productions). Jasmine has also featured in over 30 productions as a member of the BBC Radio Drama Company.

### Noof McEwan JADEN
Theatre includes: *Wildfire* (Hampstead Theatre), *Richard III* (Cockpit Theatre), *A Midsummer Night's Dream* (Almeida Theatre), *Respect* (Birmingham Rep), *Rendition Monologues* (Sheffield Crucible). Film and television includes: *Teen Spirit* (Automatik Entertainment), *The Mummy* (K/O Paper Products), *Leave to Remain* (Indefinite Films), *The Conversations* (Al Productions), *Extraordinary Rendition* (Ultra Films LTD), *Weird Love* (Future Proof Films), *Chaos Black* (Future Proof Films), *Love, Lies and Records* (BBC1), *Vera* (ITV1), *Holby City* (BBC), *Taggart* (ITV), *River City* (BBC).

### Tom Clegg GUNSHOT-WOUND RABBIT
Theatre includes: *Think of England*, *Posh* (Nottingham Playhouse), *Shakespeare in Love* (West End), *A Marked Man* (HighTide), *Outside on the Street* (Arcola), *Solid Air* (Theatre Royal Plymouth), *DNA* (Hull Truck and UK National Tour). Film and Television includes: *A Discovery of Witches*, *The Trip to Spain*, *And Then There Were None* (BBC), *Doctors* (BBC).

### Abrahim Jarman BURNT-FUR RABBIT
Theatre includes: *Aladdin* (Maidenhead Panto). Film and Television includes: *The Let's Go Club* (CBBC), *Bitesize Shakespeare* (BBC), *Living It* (CBBC), *Holby City* (BBC), *The Bill* (Talkback Thames), *Casualty* (BBC).

### Josh Azouz Writer

Josh's debut play *The Mikvah Project* premiered at the Yard Theatre in London and became the best-selling show in the theatre's history at that time. It is currently under option for a production in New York. He has completed writers groups at the Royal Court and The Bush, and is an associate artist for The Yard and MUJU (Muslim-Jewish Theatre Company.) Josh has directed for The Tricycle, Oval House & Library Theatre. Highlights include the Edinburgh festival show *The Man Who Almost Killed Himself* which was filmed for the BBC iplayer and Odeons nationwide. He also co-created the world's first comedy show on exercise bikes - *Sink or Shpin*. Josh is currently on attachment to the National Theatre. Other theatre includes *Victoria's Knickers* (NYT); *10,000 Smarties* (Oxford Festival of Arts/ Three Street Productions). As Writer/ Director: *Come In! Sit Down!* (Tricycle); *The Bike* (Royal Court/Pimlico Playground). As Director: *The Man Who Almost Killed Himself* (Summerhall Edinburgh); *Spur Of The Moment, The Good Person of Sichuan* (ALRA); *The Thunders* (As Associate, Giffords Circus); *On Dis Ting* (Oval House); *Gargantua* (Capitol Theatre, Manchester Metropolitan University/ Norfox Young People's Theatre); *Sinbad* (Freedom Studios / The Roundhouse).

### Ned Bennett Director

Ned Bennett is an award-winning theatre director, who trained at the Royal Court, the National Theatre and LAMDA. His work includes the Evening Standard Award-winning *An Octoroon*, which opened at the Orange Tree Theatre in Spring 2017 and will transfer to the National Theatre's Dorfman Theatre in Summer 2018. Ned directed the Bruntwood Prize-winning *Yen* at the Manchester Royal Exchange which transferred to the Royal Court in 2016, and *Pomona* which was commissioned by the Royal Welsh College of Music & Drama and transferred to the Orange Tree, and then to the National Theatre. *Pomona* and *Yen* won Ned the UK Theatre Best Director award in 2015. *Pomona* won four Off-West End awards: Best Director, Best Production, Best New Play and Best Lighting Design. Ned also developed and directed a scratch performance of *Brixton Rock* with care-leavers for The Big House in 2017, based on the book of the same name by Alex Wheatle.

### Max Johns Designer

Max Johns trained in theatre design at Bristol Old Vic Theatre School and was the recipient of a BBC performing arts fellowship in 2015. Prior to this he worked for a number of years as a designer in Germany. Recent designer credits include: *Yellowman* (Young Vic), *Baddies* (Synergy Theatre Project), *Kes* (West

Yorkshire Playhouse), *Fidelio* (London Philharmonic Orchestra and Royal Festival Hall), *Twelfth Night* (The Orange Tree), *Hamlet* and *All's Well That Ends Well* (Shakespeare at the Tobacco Factory), *The Merry Owls* (The V&A Museum), *An Elephant in the Garden* (Poonamallee Productions), *A Christmas Carol* (The Old Red Lion), *Infinity Pool* (Theatre West and Tobacco Factory Theatres), *Enron, The Eleventh Hour* and *Our Town* (The Egg), *Life Raft, Medusa* and *Under a Cardboard Sea* (Bristol Old Vic).

**Giles Thomas** Composer and Sound Designer
Current and forthcoming projects include: *The Importance Of Being Earnest* (UK Tour 2018); *The Almighty Sometimes* (Royal Exchange); *A Streetcar Named Desire* (Southampton Nuffield). Composer & Sound Design credits include: *Wait Until Dark* (UK Tour); *Handbagged* (Theatre by the Lake); *Death Of A Salesman* (Royal and Derngate); *How My Light In Spent* (Royal Exchange); *Othello* (Tobacco Factory, Bristol); *Wish List, Yen* (Royal Exchange & Royal Court); *Contractions* (Sheffield Theatres); *Correspondence* (Old Red Lion); *I See You* (Royal Court); *Pomona* (National Theatre, Royal Exchange Theatre & Orange Tree Theatre); *Sparks* (Old Red Lion); *The Titanic Orchestra, This Will End Badly, Allie* (Edinburgh); *Little Malcolm And His Struggle Against The Eunuchs* (Southwark Playhouse); *Outside Mullingar* (Theatre Royal Bath); *Back Down* (Birmingham Rep); *Wolf From The Door, Primetime, Mint, Pigeons, Death Tax, The President Has Come To See You* (Royal Court); *Lie With Me* (Talawa); *The Sound Of Yellow* (Young Vic); *Take A Deep Breath And Breathe, The Street* (Oval House Theatre); *Stop Kiss* (Leicester Square Theatre). Sound Design credits include: *Hijabi Monologues* (Bush Theatre); *Disco Pigs* (Trafalgar Studios & Irish Rep Theatre NY); *The Ugly One, A Dark Night In Dalston* (Park Theatre); *Dyl* (Old Red Lion); *What Shadows* (Birmingham Rep & Park Theatre); *They Drink It In The Congo* (Almeida); *The Sugar-coated Bullets Of The Bourgeoisie* (Arcola, Hightide Festival); *Decades* (The Brit School for Performing Arts); *The Snow Queen* (Southampton Nuffield & Northampton Royal & Derngate); *Orson's Shadow* (Southwark Playhouse); *Defect* (Arts Ed); *Betrayal* (I Fagiolini, UK Tour); *A Harlem Dream* (Young Vic); *Khandan* (Birmingham Rep, Royal Court); *Superior Donuts* (Southwark Playhouse); *Three Men In A Boat* (Original Theatre Company, UK Tour); *King John* (Union Theatre); *Its About Time* (Nabokov Theatre Company, Hampstead Theatre); *Shoot/Get Treasure/Repeat* (Royal Court, Gate Theatre, Out of Joint, Paines Plough, National Theatre); *House Of Agnes* (Paines Plough). Associate Sound Designer on: *Ma Raineys Black Bottom* (National Theatre); *Henry IV* (Donmar Warehouse & Tour); *Henry V* (Michael Grandage Company, West End); *1984* (West End, UK Tour). Music Producer on: *An*

*Appointment With The Wickerman* (National Theatre of Scotland). Screen credits include: *Aurelia* (Jade Edwards) *Ident* (Anaya Productions); *Cern Hadron Collider Exhibition* (Science Museum); *Street Spirit* (Tom Bailey); *Last Of The Oaks* (Luis Baron). Giles was nominated for Best Sound Designer at the Off West End Awards 2015 for his work on *Pomona.*

### Jess Bernberg Lighting Designer

Lighting Design credits include: *Dungeness* (Nuffield Southampton Theatres), *Devil with the Blue Dress* (Bunker Theatre), *Split* (Vault Festival), *Love and Information* (Nuffield Southampton Theatres), *FCUK'D* (Bunker Theatre), *Ajax* (The Space), *The Blue Hour of Natalie Barney* (Arcola Theatre), *The Death of Ivan Ilyich* (Merton Arts Space), *And the Rest of Me Floats* (Birmingham Rep, Rose Lipman Building), *And Here I Am* (UK Tour), *The Poetry We Make* (Vault Festival, RADA, Rosemary Branch, Old Red Lion), *WAYWARD* (Vault Festival), *The Dowager's Oyster* (Arcola Theatre), *This is Matty, and He is Fucked* (Winemaker's Club), *Youkali: The Pursuit of Happiness* (Arcola Theatre), *Flux: Shadowlines* (King's Place), *The Selfish Giant* (Arcola Theatre), *SQUIRM* (King's Head, Theatre503, Bread & Roses Theatre, C Venues), *Glitter & Tears* (Bread & Roses Theatre, theSpace UK), *After the Dance* (Upstairs at the Gatehouse). As an Assistant Lighting Designer: *The Tale of Two Cities* (Regent's Park Open Air Theatre), *Fox on the Fairway* (Queen's Theatre Hornchurch). For Guildhall: *Balm in Gilead*, *The Same Deep Water As Me*, *August.* On Placement: *The Ferryman* (Royal Court Theatre), *Nuclear War* (Royal Court Theatre), *Ink* (Almeida Theatre). Jess is also the 2018 Laboratory Associate Lighting Designer at Nuffield Southampton Theatres and received the Association of Lighting Designer's Francis Reid Award for Lighting in 2017.

### Sophie Parrott CDG Casting Director

Theatre credits include: *An Octoroon* (Orange Tree Theatre & National Theatre); Liverpool Everyman Company 2018; *Old Fools* (Southwark Playhouse); *Winter Solstice* (Actors Touring Company); *The March On Russia* (Orange Tree Theatre); *The Claim* (Shoreditch Town Hall & National Tour); *All The President's Men?* (National Theatre); *This Beautiful Future* (The Yard Theatre); *Death Of A Salesman* (Royal & Derngate Theatre, Northampton & Tour); *Wish List* (Royal Court, London and Royal Exchange, Manchester); *A Streetcar Named Desire* (co-casting director, Royal Exchange, Manchester); *Bird* (Sherman Cymru & Royal Exchange, Manchester); *Yen* (Royal Court, London and Royal Exchange, Manchester); *My Mother Said I Never Should* (St

James Theatre); *A Midsummer Night's Dream* (Everyman); *Britannia Waves the Rules* (UK Tour); *Pomona* (additional casting, National Theatre); *The Crocodile* (Manchester International Festival) and *Billy Liar* (Royal Exchange, Manchester). As Casting Associate and Assistant, television credits include: *Howards End, Delicious, Rillington Place, Thirteen, Call the Midwife* (four series), *Silent Witness* (two series), *The Game, Esio Trot, Mr Stink, WPC56, The Preston Passion, The Night Watch, Holby City* (four series), *The Riots: In Their Own Words, Undeniable.* As Casting Director, television credits include: *Doctors.* Film credits include: *The Secret Agent, Whirlpool, A Street Cat Named Bob* (as Casting Associate).

### Seb Cannings Production Manager
Theatre Credits as Production Manager include: *Puma FUTURE VAULT* (Ambika P3), *Wilde Creatures* (Vaudeville Theatre), *Around The World in 80 Days* (UK Tour). As Assistant Production Manager: *Dick Whittington* (Palladium Theatre), *La Strada* (UK Tour), *The Glass Menagerie* (Duke of York's Theatre), *In With A Bang* (Humber Marina, Hull City of Culture), *Peter Pan* (The Alhambra Theatre), *Cinderella* (Palladium Theatre), *6 Day* (Lee Valley VeloPark London / Madison), *Harry Potter and the Cursed Child Parts I & II* (Palace Theatre).

### Edwina Allen Stage Manager on the Book
Edwina trained at ALRA. She has a career spanning 12 years with a wide range of experience across theatre and live events. Theatre credits as DSM include: *Goosebumps Alive* and *Alice's Adventures Underground* (The Vaults), *Dirty Great Love Story* (Arts, West End). As Stage Manager: *Trestle* (Papatango, Southwark Playhouse), *No Villain* (Old Red Lion, Trafalgar Studios). Edwina has also worked on stadium ceremonies including: Doha Asian Games 2006, Vancouver Winter Olympics 2010, Arab Games 2011, London Olympics & Paralympics 2012, Glasgow Commonwealth Games 2014.

### Kate Clement Assistant Stage Manager
Kate Clement is a Prop Supervisor and ASM based in London. Kate has previously worked at The Bush, Young Vic, Southwark Playhouse and Crucible Theatres.

# The Yard Theatre

In 2011 a group of volunteers, led by Jay Miller, used recycled and reclaimed materials to convert a disused warehouse in Hackney Wick, into a theatre, bar and kitchen. They called it The Yard.

A multi-award winning theatre, The Yard offers a space for artists to grow new stories and new ideas, and for audiences to access outstanding new work.

*"One of London's most essential theatres"* Lyn Gardner, *Guardian*

The Yard has rapidly established itself as a theatrical necessity with a reputation for upending theatrical traditions, and injecting creativity and fearlessness into wider contemporary culture.

The Yard Theatre is committed to:
1. Exposing stories from unheard voices.
2. Interrogating the process of writing for performance.
3. Discovering and developing artists.

In The Yard's short existence it has had significant success. This includes transfers to the National Theatre for *Beyond Caring* and *Chewing Gum Dreams*, and numerous awards including the final Peter Brook Empty Space Award (2017). Success has also led to partnerships with leading theatres and organisations; recent partners include the Young Vic, Royal Court Theatre, National Theatre and HighTide Festival Theatre.

*"The most important theatre in east London"* Time Out

Alongside the theatre, The Yard is fast becoming one of London's most diverse and exciting venues for experiencing new music, filling the bar with people dancing until the early hours.

The Yard Theatre also manages Hub67, a community centre in Hackney Wick - a place for neighbours, young people and creative ideas. Through Hub67, The Yard is exploring what role a theatre can play in its community. It offers free creative activities to local residents and gives young people the opportunity to see theatre, learn about performance and make work for The Yard stage as part of Yard Young Artists.

The Yard Theatre brings artists and audiences together in an exciting environment where anything becomes possible.


Recent productions include:

**Beyond Caring** by Alexander Zeldin, which transferred to the National Theatre and has completed an international tour ("quietly devastating" ★★★★ *Guardian*).

**The Mikvah Project** written by Josh Azouz, directed by Jay Miller, which played a sold-out, extended run ("Every moment feels rich with meaning" ★★★★ *Time Out*).

**LINES** written by Pamela Carter, directed by Jay Miller, which received substantial critical acclaim ("directed with finesse by The Yard's properly talented artistic director Jay Miller" ★★★★ *Time Out*).

**Made Visible** written by Deborah Pearson, directed by Stella Odunlami, which sparked lively debate around white privilege ("a serious examination of racism and the inadequacies of liberalism" ★★★★ *Guardian*).

**Removal Men** written by M. J. Harding, with Jay Miller, which received two Off West End Award nominations for Best New Play and Most Promising Playwright ("Jay Miller's mesmerically intense production uses music to carve out a space for huge ideas" ★★★★ *Time Out*).

**This Beautiful Future** written by Rita Kalnejais, directed by Jay Miller, was, due to popular demand, the first show to be remounted at The Yard following a sell-out, critically acclaimed and extended run. ("Nothing short of mesmerising" ★★★★★ *The Stage*).

**www.theyardtheatre.co.uk**

# The Yard Theatre

**Supporters**
Arts Council England
The Kirsh Foundation
Garfield Weston Foundation
Patrick and Helena Frost Foundation

**Thank You To All Our Friends & Guardians Including:**
Francesco Curto & Chantal Rivest, Joanna Kennedy, Greg Delaney, Paul Miller & Mary Shaw, Ian & Janet Edmondson, The David Pearlman Foundation, Laura Hodgson, Ben Rogers, Nick Hytner, Robin Saphra, Melanie Johnson, Anna Vaughan & Dan Fletcher, Archie & Carolyn Ward

**Thanks**
Like all our shows, *Buggy Baby* owes its existence to the people and organisations who have lent their time, their energies and their stuff.

We would like to thank: The Orange Tree Theatre, Whitelight, Chauvet, Islington Arts Factory, Amera Otaifa

*For Mandy*

# BUGGY BABY

*Buggy Baby* was first performed at The Yard, London, on 7 March 2018. The cast was as follows:

| | |
|---|---|
| NUR | Hoda Bentaher |
| JADEN | Noof McEwan |
| BABY AYA | Jasmine Jones |
| GUNSHOT-WOUND RABBIT | Tom Clegg |
| BURNT-FUR RABBIT | Abrahim Jarman |

| | |
|---|---|
| *Director* | Ned Bennett |
| *Designer* | Max Johns |
| *Lighting Designer* | Jess Bernberg |
| *Composer and Sound Designer* | Giles Thomas |

## Acknowledgements

I'd like to thank the following people who helped me figure out this play. Najib Alhakimi, Alice Birch, Georgina Bednar, Bernadette Cahill, Nadia Clifford, Souad Faress, Bettrys Jones, Youssef Kerkour, Serena Manteghi, Hamish Pirie, Ashley Scott Layton, Giles Smart, Louise Stephens, Parth Thakerar, Zubin Varla, Nic Wass. The Royal Court Writers Group.

I'd especially like to thank Ned Bennett and Jay Miller for their extensive dramaturgical support. The Yard gang. The fearless actors and creative team. And lastly Zadie... for more recent inspiration.

## Characters

NUR, *eighteen*
JADEN, *mid-thirties*
BABY AYA

TWO RABBITS/MEN

## Author's Note

Baby Aya wears an NHS-prescribed helmet. The sort given to babies to correct a misshapen or flat head. The character might be played by an older woman.

The actors are should speak in their own natural accent. On the odd occasion when they speak English, they should adopt an accent because it's their second language.

**Note on the Text**

Words in brackets ( ) should be played by the actor, not said out loud.

… indicates a hesitation, unspoken or unfinished thought, or when a character is searching for a word.

A forward slash (/) indicates the point at which the next speaker interrupts.

The lines in **BOLD** should be spoken directly to the audience.

Spaces in between lines are invitations for longer pauses or signifiers of time passing.

*This text went to press before the end of rehearsals and so may differ slightly from the play as performed.*

## Prologue

*The house lights are still on.*

*A damp room.*
*A wardrobe. A sink. Two mattresses on the floor.*
*People shouldn't live here.*

*From the wardrobe we hear:*

NUR. They've gone.

JADEN. Shh.

NUR. They've definitely gone.

JADEN. How do you know!?

NUR. I can't hear them.

JADEN. Maybe they're waiting for us to come out.

NUR. We're talking quite loudly they'd hear *us*!

JADEN. Shush then!

NUR. I can't feel my legs.

JADEN. Stay still.

> NUR *creeps out of the wardrobe. She's sixteen years old.*

NUR!

> NUR *looks at the audience.*

> *A* MAN *enters the room.*

> *Beat.*

NUR *runs.* MAN *chases.*

*Across the stage, through the seats, up the balcony, out the doors… we might even hear him chase her around the bar.*

*At one point during the chase the* MAN *puts two fingers above his head and exposes his front teeth like a rabbit. Blackout.*


*Spotlight on the wardrobe door.* JADEN *opens it and looks at us.*

JADEN. **IN THE MIDDLE OF THE NIGHT THEY FLED THEIR WAR-TORN HOME. FIVE JOURNEYED THROUGH AFRICA. FOUR CROSSED THE MEDITERRANEAN. THREE TOOK A LORRY THROUGH EUROPE...**
**JADEN WOULD TELL YOU THE NAME OF HIS HOME BUT IT NO LONGER EXISTS.**


*Spotlight on* NUR, *who pauses mid-chase, breathing hard.*

NUR. **NUR DIDN'T THINK THIS TYPE OF SHIT HAPPENED IN LONDON. SHE THOUGHT *RUNNING* BELONGED TO THE PAST. THANK GOD SHE KEPT HER TRAINERS.**

NUR *runs off.*
*Blackout.*

## One

*The room has an addition. A baby.*

BABY AYA *is asleep in her buggy. She wears a helmet.*

JADEN *is sweeping the room.*

NUR *enters, aged eighteen. Takes off her shoes. Watches*
BABY AYA *sleep.*

NUR. Here. Got you something.

> NUR *throws a blue plastic bag to* JADEN. *He looks inside.*
>
> *Beat.*

JADEN. From where?

NUR. There's an Ethiopian restaurant near college.

JADEN. I don't like you hanging around those types of places.

NUR. It's a restaurant, not a brothel.

JADEN. I didn't know it was legal here.

NUR. It isn't.

JADEN. Nur!

> JADEN *looks at the audience.*

Some of them might be police.

NUR. Unlikely. This lot actually look like they're down for a
chew. Unless they're after something stronger.

> JADEN *and* NUR *smile at the audience.*
> JADEN *looks again in the blue bag.*

JADEN. How did you know they had leaves?

NUR. I went in for a can of Sprite and the guy behind the counter kept talking. Talking so much I thought his jaw was going to drop off, or run away, but no the jaw stay fixed and he talked about the weather and that he's been staring at the same road for time and it's doing his brain and that his son swims every day and wants to go Olympics which I thought was original cos there can't have been many Ethiopian Olympic swimmers.

JADEN *inspects the leaves*.

JADEN. They're a different texture.

NUR. I'm sure they taste the same.

JADEN. How did you pay?

NUR. I appealed to the Ethiopian's soul.

JADEN. Generous man to give you leaves for free.

NUR. Oh he didn't. Told me to fuck off, so I had to borrow some money off a girl from the year below.

JADEN. Borrow? How much!?

NUR. Twelve pounds.

JADEN. Twelve pounds!? How will we pay her back!?

NUR. Relax, she's a friend.

JADEN *drops the bag*.

Thought leaves would cheer you up.

JADEN. The leaves smell, they shouldn't smell.

NUR. And give you energy, for a / job.

JADEN. If they've been tampered with they'll make you do crazy things. I once tried to dance with a scorpion.

NUR. Can I have some then?

JADEN. Didn't you hear what I just said!?

NUR. I like dancing.

JADEN. Well you can't chew.

NUR. Why?

JADEN. I just don't want you to.

NUR. Girls doing one thing, boys doing another?

JADEN. I didn't mean it like / that.

NUR. You sound like a dinosaur. And we all know what
happened to dinosaurs.

NUR *approaches the bag*.

JADEN. Chew now and you'll never get for college.

NUR *pauses*.

How was college?

NUR. Quite amusing. In English we reworked a fairytale. I
wrote one called *Snow White and the Seven-Year-Old Dwarf*.

JADEN. What did the teacher think?

NUR. She liked it cos it was inclusive.

JADEN *looks at the bag*.

You scared or something?

JADEN. . . .
Leaves distort time.
Make you see the whole world whilst remaining still.

NUR. *Okay.*

JADEN. Root you.

NUR. Root you?

JADEN. As if your feet are nailed to the floor.

NUR. Whoa.

JADEN. Why did you bring them into our home?

NUR. I just thought, you know, a gift.

*A tense pause.*

Twister?

NUR *and* JADEN *play Twister.*


JADEN *walks away from the game.*

NUR. We done then?

JADEN. Sometimes I'd chew with Yusrah.

NUR. Oh so Yusrah was allowed to chew.

JADEN. We were teenagers.

NUR. Before you were married!?

JADEN. Yeah.

NUR. Naughty.

*Beat.*

JADEN *pops a leaf into his mouth.*

*Beat.*

I thought it's just like coffee.

JADEN. It is just like coffee.

NUR. I've been drinking coffee since I was ten.

*Beat.*
JADEN *offers* NUR *the bag. She puts a leaf in her mouth.*
*They chew.*

Not feeling anything.

JADEN. It takes a while.

JADEN *stuffs more and more leaves into his mouth.* NUR
*follows.*
*After a while they each have a bulging cheek.*

JADEN *looks at* NUR *chewing*.

Your parents will be thrashing about.

NUR. They won't be watching.

JADEN. How do you know?

NUR. They don't have eyes.

JADEN. The dead don't need eyes to see.

NUR. The dead don't need eyes cos they're dead.

JADEN. You an expert on the afterlife?

NUR. There is no afterlife.

JADEN. That must be depressing for you.

NUR. Whatever.
Time for English. I've been slack.

JADEN. That's one way to ruin the chew.

NUR. Repeat after me. (*With accent.*) I'm hardworking,
trustworthy, punctual.

JADEN (*with stronger accent*). I'm hardworking, trustworthy,
punctual.

NUR. Excellent. (*With accent.*) It would be an honour to clean
your toilet.

JADEN (*with stronger accent*). It would be an honour to clean –
(*No accent.*) oh go away.

NUR (*with accent*). I'm okay with skidmarks.

JADEN. Stop!

NUR. You can't keep doing Mustafa's weeds for what he's
paying.

JADEN. Weeds!? Come and see the Eden I'm creating.
Orchids, geraniums, salvias. A rockery! Water feature!
Compost!

NUR. Go for the job tomorrow.

*Beat.*

JADEN. I'll try.

NUR *smiles.*
*Spits out her leaves into her hand and puts them in the bin.*

NUR. Very bitter.

JADEN. Drink something fizzy.

NUR *opens the fridge. Drinks a can of something fizzy.*
*Pause.*
NUR *looks at the sleeping* BABY AYA.

NUR. Was she smiley today?

JADEN. Like always. She's a happy little girl.

NUR. Mm.

JADEN. Babies don't need much.

NUR. No.

JADEN. Just attention.

NUR. She's quite yellow.

*Beat.*

On the bus I think about her face. The cheeks I could eat. But when I get home I don't... it's like I don't recognise her.

JADEN. You'll be tired from college.

NUR (*casual*). I might be a barbarian.

JADEN. Eh!?

NUR. Just something I've been thinking.

*Pause.*

JADEN. Did I ever tell you about the time I had tea with the Queen?

NUR *gives* JADEN *a look.*

The Queen invites me to tea at Buckingham Palace.

NUR. Course she does.

JADEN. We eat cucumber sandwiches, scones, cakes. That long
chocolate sausage with cream in the middle. We have a nice
chat. About the weather mostly. And the Queen is the perfect
host, the way she pushes food it's like we're family. I feel
guilty for eating so much but then I try something called
meringue and the guilt passes. After we finish, the Queen
picks up a little bell. Rings it twice. Two servants enter the
room. The first servant kneels down and holds a bucket. The
second servant puts two fingers down the Queen's throat.
She vomits up the entire tea. I scream! Everyone else goes
quiet. The Queen slowly lifts her face from the bucket.
Looks me in the eyes. And burps.

NUR *(mocking). Is it.*

JADEN. True story.

NUR *(chuckling).* The fucking Queen.

> NUR *gives the audience a look.*
> JADEN *stuffs more leaves into his mouth.*
> NUR *and* JADEN *exchange charged looks.*
> *Desire breaks down the doors.*

**Two**

*On the floor is the blue plastic bag with the leftover leaves.*
BABY AYA *is awake in her buggy, looking at us.*

JADEN *enters pushing an enormous box. He pushes it slowly
across the room. We're in Buster Keaton territory here.* JADEN
*opens the box. Takes out an industrial heater. Plugs the industrial
heater into the wall. An orange glow washes over the room.*

*The heater is very close to the bag.*

BABY AYA *smiles at* JADEN.
JADEN *begins to goof around.*
*A game emerges.*
BABY AYA *squeals in delight.*

*Mid-game,* BABY AYA*'s face becomes still and serious.*

*Then it goes very red.*
*She's pushing out a poo.*

BABY AYA *finishes. She smiles at* JADEN, *pleased with herself.*

**Three**

*The room has a new addition. A giant tree.*
*The tree touches the ceiling. It is surrounded by lights and the industrial heater. The tree has an artificial colour.*

NUR. **WHEN THE LEAVES YOU BOUGHT GROW INTO A GIANT TREE, IT'S TIME TO MAKE SOME MOTHERFUCKING DECISIONS.**

NUR *and* BABY AYA *stare at each other.*

NUR *knocks on the wardrobe door.*
JADEN *steps out of the wardrobe.*

Alright?

JADEN *nods.*

JADEN *gets a can of tuna. Starts to prise it open with a rusty tin opener.*

JADEN. Mustafa has a rabbit problem.

NUR. A rabbit problem.

JADEN. They've taken over. They're digging up the flowerbeds.

NUR. Rabbits in Knightsbridge?

JADEN. Uh-huh.

NUR. Don't the foxes eat them?

JADEN. Apparently not. Knightsbridge foxes just sunbathe.
I googled a deterrent.
Human hair.

NUR *is looking at* BABY AYA.

Nur?

NUR. Yeah.

JADEN. Human hair. Puts the rabbits off. They don't like the smell. So the plan is to create a perimeter fence of hair around the flowers. That will stop the bastards. They think they can just plunder the earth, destroy civilisation, take over the world, where is their empathy?

NUR. Aren't they rabbits?

JADEN. They're rabbits alright but rabbits with black souls. So I need your hair.

NUR. Sounds a bit dark.

JADEN. Fancy donating?

NUR. Huh?

JADEN. You'd look beautiful with short hair.

NUR. You're a joker if you think you're touching my hair.

*Beat.*

JADEN. How was college?

NUR. I don't wanna talk about it.

*Beat.*

JADEN. Well, the wise woman ignores the birdsong and listens to the wind.

NUR. For fuck's sake.

JADEN. When a preacher farts only a fundamentalist shits.

NUR. Enough.

JADEN. D'you know what it means?

NUR. I don't care.

JADEN. It means don't be so literal. So if I was to say let me
    have some of your hair, you might say 'sure'

NUR. Show me your eyes.

JADEN. Let's eat.

NUR. They're red.

JADEN. I'm tired.

NUR. Your eyes are red and your pupils are like an oil slick!

JADEN. Eat.

NUR. I'm not hungry.

JADEN. Great, more for me.

NUR. I'm starving!

JADEN. You prefer seawater and grass?

NUR. Tuna in brine. There's not much in it.

JADEN. The way you talk about starving – it's a disgrace.

NUR. What time did you start chewing?

JADEN. I'm not chewing! There is nothing in my mouth!

NUR (*shakes her head*). We made a deal.

JADEN. I cooked dinner you should be impressed.

NUR. You promised you wouldn't start till four.

JADEN. So I had a little chew. The room hasn't burnt down.
    The plant hasn't swallowed Aya.

NUR. YOU DON'T CHEW TILL I COME HOME.

NUR *approaches* BABY AYA.
BABY AYA *looks away.*

She won't look at me.

JADEN. Smile at her she's a baby!

NUR *smiles at* BABY AYA.

Little gazelle where's that smile? Where's that smile?

BABY AYA *gives* JADEN *a big smile. They might reprise
their game from Scene Two.*
NUR *smiles again at* BABY AYA.
BABY AYA *scowls.*
NUR *walks off. Picks up a hula hoop. Spins it around her
stomach. Looks at* JADEN *and* BABY AYA.

NUR *tosses away the hoop.*

NUR. There's a boy at college that looks at me. Looks at me a
lot since I waxed my lip.

NUR *looks at* JADEN *for a response.*

One of the brown girls I mentor has a beard. I told her to
wax it but she wasn't having any of it. She dyed it. It went
purple. School's *so* over for her now.
But getting my lip waxed has given me a real edge.

NUR *looks at* JADEN *for a response.*

JADEN. Would the girl with the purple beard consider shaving
it off?

NUR. I don't think so. She'll get stubble.

JADEN. Pity. Could use it for my fence.

NUR *gives* JADEN *a look.*

*Beat.*

NUR. You gonna have a word with the boy that looks at me?

*Beat.*

Do you look at women?

JADEN. I don't know any women.

NUR. Maybe you should meet one. Go on a date.

JADEN. Okay.

NUR. Download one of those apps. You'll need a photo and a bio.

JADEN. Right.

NUR. I reckon you'll go down very well. You're not ugly and although on first impressions people will think you've got large chunks of your personality missing, you've actually got a lot going for you. Drug addict, refugee, can't speak English – what a catch.

JADEN. Create one for me then.

NUR. Nah. You best keep rubbing yourself off on your mattress.

*In silence* NUR *and* JADEN *eat their blocks of tuna. Perhaps with some khubz (large pitta bread). They eat with their right hands.*

*A* RABBIT *with a gunshot wound to the head enters. Only* JADEN *sees him.*

JADEN. So what about cutting your hair?

NUR. I like my hair. Don't you?

JADEN. Yeah, but I'd prefer it shorter.

JADEN *takes out some large scissors.*

NUR. Er back off with those.

JADEN. A woman with a shaved head is trendy no?

NUR. Not with my features.

JADEN. Give me your hair!

> NUR *moves away from* JADEN *and unwittingly closer to the* RABBIT. *The* RABBIT *runs off.*

> *Beat.*

NUR. You may be able to exist like this.
Dreaming about rabbits.
But I won't.
And she can't.

> *Beat.*

JADEN. What do you want from me darling?

NUR. (EVERYTHING!?) A cot. A cot so she can lie on her tummy.

JADEN. I'm saving up. Just a few more weeks. Do you hear that little gazelle.

> JADEN *walks towards the wardrobe.*

NUR. So that's it, you're disappearing for the night now are you?

JADEN. You can spend some time with Aya.

NUR. I know I can spend some time!

JADEN. Calm down.

NUR. You think you're the only one who knows how to be with her!?

> NUR *approaches* BABY AYA.
> BABY AYA *eyeballs* NUR, *daring to be picked up.*

JADEN. So pick her up.

NUR. I am picking her up!

JADEN. If you don't want to hold her, lie her on the floor.

NUR. The floor, look at the floor, what planet are you on!?

> *Beat.*

JADEN. Are you jealous?

NUR. Why would I be jealous!?

JADEN. Because you can't hold (her)

*Beat.*

NUR. One day you might wake up and find us gone.

*Beat.*

JADEN *rips off a handful of leaves from the tree. Sulks off into the wardrobe.*
NUR *and* BABY AYA *alone.*
*They're like nervous teenagers on a first date.*

(*To* BABY AYA.) A couple of years ago I went on a school trip to Stonehenge. On the coach journey back we stopped at a service station, most of the class bought sweets but I bought thirty bottles of water. An hour later everyone was thirsty, sweets do that to you, I think it's the salt. I sold the water bottles at triple the price. Made a killing. Do you think I should cut my hair short?

BABY AYA. Lift me out the buggy.

*Beat.*

Do I smell?

NUR. Like peach.

BABY AYA. Cool. Thought I sharted.
So lift me?

NUR. I can't.

*Beat.*

BABY AYA. Did you speak to the teachers about our situation?

NUR. Yeah.

BABY AYA. ?

NUR. I don't want them involved.

BABY AYA. Then you might as well sack off college.

*Beat.*

NUR. They actually asked me to join the college council.

BABY AYA. Is that a bit like the milk monitor?

NUR. Nah. You make decisions.

BABY AYA. Baller. What powers we talking? Capital punishment.

NUR. Not powers, more like responsibilities.

BABY AYA. Yawn.

NUR. Is it a distraction from ideas?

BABY AYA. What ideas?

NUR. Like selling marked-up bottles of water… times a thousand.

NUR *sings a line from 'We've Gotta Get Out of this Place'*
*by The Animals.*
BABY AYA *sings a line back.*
NUR *and* BABY AYA *sing a line together.*

BABY AYA. You'll have to sell your body.

NUR. Aya!

BABY AYA. I'd do anything to not sleep in this buggy, and if that means you lying on your back or giving a few blowjobs –

NUR. That's not gonna happen!

BABY AYA. Oldest profession in the world?

NUR. Shut up.

BABY AYA. Okay.

*Beat.*

College council hey.

NUR. Mm.

BABY AYA. I'm not sure I'll make college. I'm not sure I'll even make nursery.

NUR. Course you'll make it.

BABY AYA. Isn't education a Zionist plot to stop us having babies?

NUR. Only the uneducated talk like that.

BABY AYA. Who's my dad?

NUR. We've been through this.

BABY AYA. Let's go through it again.

*Beat.*

There's bits of him inside me cos sometimes I say things you've never said.

NUR. ...

BABY AYA. Shame you can't cut me in half. Cut out the half from my dad, and flush it down the toilet. Then we could forget there ever was a dad.

NUR. You've got a violent imagination for a baby.

BABY AYA. I've seen some terrible things.

*Beat.*

NUR. One day we'll live in a house, and it'll be warm, and the fridge will be full, and you'll have your own bedroom, with thick walls, and a lock on the door, and a cot with a mobile that hangs from above and plays music and lights up. And we'll have bookshelves. And a TV. And there'll be a garden, with a pond full of fish. Not shitty goldfish, but big fish, like actual tuna.

BABY AYA. When's that life starting?

NUR. Soon.

BABY AYA. Will Jaden come with?

NUR. Course.

BABY AYA. Maybe he belongs in a special home.

NUR.…?

BABY AYA. Call a doctor or policeman to come fetch him.

NUR. No. He just needs *us*.

BABY AYA. I think we're better off as a two.

NUR. Aya I can't… I won't…

BABY AYA. It's cool, I understand, we don't have the history yet.

*Beat.*

Skip college tomorrow.

NUR. If only you were small enough to keep in my pocket.

BABY AYA. Sounds claustrophobic.

NUR. We'd be together always.

BABY AYA. Why don't you quit college, steal a car, and drive us off into the sunset?

NUR. I can't drive.

BABY AYA. Sit me on your lap. I'll do the wheel. You do the accelerator.

NUR *smiles*.

Remember when I was born?

NUR. Not really.

BABY AYA. You used to be home all the time. I could tell from your voice. Sometimes not even your voice just your breath. I loved that, you breathing on me. It was nearly as good as the womb.

NUR. If I join the council I'd get to meet lots of useful people and it would look incredible on my CV and just basically we'd all have a much better future.

*Beat.*

BABY AYA. So be it.

NUR. Really?

BABY AYA. You go girl.

NUR. On most days I'll be home at the usual time but on Wednesdays I'd have a meeting. So it'd be more like, 5 p.m.

BABY AYA. So that's another hour with the resident schizo.

NUR. He's not a schizo –

BABY AYA. Perhaps not the textbook definition but he is two people.

NUR. SHUT THE FUCK UP!

BABY AYA *withdraws*.

Are you hungry?

BABY AYA *suckles on* NUR*'s breast for a long time*.

You bit me!

BABY AYA. THAT'LL FUCKING TEACH YOU!

NUR. Don't use that word!

BABY AYA. Wind me.

NUR. I'm bleeding!

BABY AYA. FUCKING WIND ME!
(*Sweetly.*) After you wind me I'll sleep.

NUR *gently pats and rubs* BABY AYA*'s back*.

NUR. Sleep? Sleep? With one eye open, always with me in your sights, and as I drift off you'll scream and scream and I'll wake up, although I was never asleep and I'll wipe your shit, and then beg you to sleep, but to spite me you won't, you'll scream and so I'll give you my breast and you'll suckle and bite and bleed me dry.
Why d'you sleep with one eye open?

BABY AYA. To look after Jaden.

NUR. He doesn't need looking after.

BABY AYA. I dunno. He often hangs out in the wardrobe and screams.

NUR. That's nothing to do with you.

BABY AYA. After, he uses my cheeks to wipe away his tears. My cheeks are so fucking soft nowadays. Wanna stroke 'em?

NUR *reaches out her hand to touch… then retracts.*

When he's finished crying he holds me to his chest. I can hear his heart. Beating fast. Just for me.

*Beat.*

NUR. From now on you sleep with your eyes closed.

BABY AYA. I'll try.
But can't promise anything.
It's freezing. I've got pins and needles from the neck down.
And sometimes, a cockroach eats my head.

NUR *looks at* BABY AYA *with inscrutable eyes.*
BABY AYA *burps.*

NUR. Good girl good girl. Bedtime.

BABY AYA. You gonna kill me in my sleep?

NUR. Aya!?

BABY AYA. I'm getting homicidal vibes.

NUR. I would never hurt –

BABY AYA. Yeah but I stop you Mum.

NUR. …

BABY AYA. Join the college council you'll be brilliant. But don't leave me here all day. I'm not a cat. Don't be a selfish fucking bitch your whole cunting life – (*Falls asleep mid-thought.*)

NUR, *frozen, watches her daughter sleep.*

**Four**

JADEN. **JADEN HAS BEEN CHEWING FOR FIVE HOURS.**

JADEN *chews*.

**IN A MOMENT HE WILL BE REUNITED WITH HIS DEAD WIFE.**

JADEN *stares at* BABY AYA.

Yusrah.
You look… ravishing.

BABY AYA *frowns*.

Don't talk like a maniac, I look a hundred.
We've all aged.
You'd think the salt water would preserve me but every passing creature stops to have a bite.

Don't cry. It was a relief…
Yusrah I'm (sorry)
Me too. For leaving too soon.
I can't believe I'm hearing your voice – (*Shamefully.*) I'd started to forget the sound.
Pay me a compliment. It can be banal.
Banal?
Something silly throwaway superficial.
I don't know what to say.
Surprise me. The afterlife is so boring.

Your breasts are astonishing?
Mm I've always had perky breasts.
Wanna motorboat?

JADEN *rubs his face in* BABY AYA's *chest. His hands hold tight onto* BABY AYA's *back*.

BABY AYA *is unsure about what is happening.*
*She giggles. The giggles grow into a laugh.*
*But something feels odd about this interaction with* JADEN.
BABY AYA *drops the laughter and looks at the audience.*

Yus?

BABY AYA *frowns.*

Yusrah?

JADEN *runs to the tree and stuffs more leaves into his*
*mouth.*

BABY AYA. What the fuck are you chewing mate?

JADEN. Come back Yus come back Yus come back.

A RABBIT *with burnt fur and a missing ear lollops onto the*
*stage. He holds a baseball bat.*

BURNT-FUR RABBIT *picks off a leaf. Chews. Looks at*
BABY AYA.

BURNT-FUR RABBIT. The men are lonely. Is she available?

**Five**

BABY AYA. **BABY AYA HAS A SECRET. TONIGHT**
**SHE'S GOING TO SHARE IT WITH MOM. WISH**
**HER LUCK.**

BABY AYA *is in a makeshift bath playing with a toy.*
NUR *washes her body with a sponge.*

NUR. You've been playing with that toy for ages.

BABY AYA. I've learnt to be imaginative with *shit.*

*Beat.*

Is my name Aya?

NUR. ?

BABY AYA. Just checking I've got it right.

NUR. You've got it right.

BABY AYA. Aya's not a nickname for Yusrah is it?

NUR. You're Aya.

BABY AYA. Who's Yusrah?

NUR. … someone else.

*Beat.*

Okay I'm gonna wash your head.

BABY AYA. Doctor said to keep it on at all times.

NUR. Most of the time.

BABY AYA. Exactly.

NUR. Isn't it itchy?

BABY AYA. It's the worst itch in the world. It's the itch you can never scratch.

NUR *tries to take off* BABY AYA*'s helmet.*
BABY AYA *flinches.*

NUR. I once broke my arm. It was in a cast for six weeks. I used to shove all sorts down it to try and get rid of the itch. Fork. Coat hanger. Pencil. Nothing really worked. But my mum wrote jokes and messages on the cast, so that whenever it felt itchy, I'd read them and laugh. I could write messages on your helmet.

BABY AYA. I can't read.

NUR. I'll read them for you.

BABY AYA. Okay cool.

NUR. Great. I'll write them after bathtime.
Gonna take off your helmet now.

BABY AYA. Will it hurt?

NUR. No, cos you're very very brave.

> NUR *delicately unstraps* BABY AYA*'s helmet and examines her head.*

BABY AYA. Is it round yet?

NUR. (No.) Nearly.

> BABY AYA *puts up her hand to feel her head.*

Don't touch it. We don't want it to get infected.

> BABY AYA *puts her hand down.*

Gonna wash it veeeery gently.

> NUR *squeezes a sponge over* BABY AYA*'s head.*

Feel good?

BABY AYA. Mmmmmmmmmm.

> NUR *washes* BABY AYA*'s head.*

> *Puts the helmet back on* BABY AYA*'s head.*

Are there holes in my back?

NUR. What?

> *There are marks on her back after* JADEN *held her when he motorboated.*

BABY AYA. How's the milk monitor going?

NUR. The *college council* is going brilliantly. Today we met a politican. I put forward an idea about education's relationship to housing.

BABY AYA. Can this politican help *us*?

NUR. I don't think so.

BABY AYA. My skin feels quite thin. Like it was made for a puncture.

NUR. There are no holes.

> *Beat.*

There are some... scratches.

BABY AYA.... scratches.

*Beat.*

Maybe I scratched myself in my sleep – like when I was newborn.

NUR. Yeah that'll be it.

BABY AYA. Although I don't think I could reach that part of my back.

NUR. Maybe the buggy did it. You know, rubbing against it.

BABY AYA. Nah. The buggy doesn't have fingernails.

*Beat.*

Scratching. Is it something I should be learning?

NUR. You making up stories again? I don't mind if you are.

BABY AYA. How did you break your arm?

NUR. A boy was running after me, in the playground, I tripped, landed on it badly.

BABY AYA. That sounds made up.

NUR. What?

BABY AYA. You say my story of being scratched sounds made up but then when I ask you a question about your arm you come out with some shit about tripping in a playground.

NUR. I said I don't mind if you make up stories.

BABY AYA. Mum you might be good at college but you're fucking dim in every other way.

NUR. Aya!

BABY AYA. I ought to have a word with that politician about the curriculum. No use teaching you to read and write, if they don't teach you how to *mother.*

NUR *walks away from the bath.*

Mum.

*Beat.*

Mum!

*Beat.*

Mum Mum Mum Mum Mu Mum Mum MUM
MUUUUUUUUUUUUUUUUUM MUM MUM MUM
MUM Mum Mummy Mummy Mummy Ma Ma Mummy
Mumma.

BABY AYA *in her agitation finds herself on her back. She is*
*splashing about, trying to lift herself up.*
BABY AYA *is starting to drown.*
NUR *runs and lifts* BABY AYA *out of the bath at the nick of*
*time.*


NUR *puts on* BABY AYA*'s nappy.*
*Gives her massage with baby oil.*
*Dresses her in a Babygro.*
*Blows a raspberry on her stomach.* BABY AYA *laughs*
*hysterically.*
*The laughs die.*

When the axe entered the woods, the trees said: oh look, the
handle is one of us. No one noticed the blade.

**Six**

BABY AYA *is asleep. Her helmet is covered in drawings,*
*henna patterns and jokes in Arabic.*

NUR. **WHEN YOU HAVE NOTHING. YOUR DREAMS**
**ARE FUEL.**

JADEN. **A RAGS-TO-RICHES IMMIGRANT-DONE-**
**GOOD STORY, STARRING –**

NUR. As they say in East London – (*With accent.*) we need to
see a man about a dog.

JADEN. I've no idea what that means but it sounds promising.

NUR. Have you ever stolen anything?

JADEN. What, like a thief?

NUR. Not big things, just little things.

JADEN. Don't be ridiculous.

NUR. You can tell me, I won't judge.

JADEN. I've never stolen anything.

NUR. When you were young, you never stole a fig from the
market?

JADEN. That's not really stealing.

NUR. So you stole a fig.

JADEN. I had friends who stole.

NUR. Which friends, my dad?

JADEN. Where's this conversation going?

NUR. We're brainstorming.

*Beat.*

JADEN (*whispering*). I might have stolen a fig.

NUR. Why are you whispering?

JADEN. We don't want to set a bad example.

NUR. She's asleep.

JADEN. She hears things.

NUR. Okay what else, we've established figs.

JADEN. I don't know… pistachio nuts.

NUR. Standard.

JADEN. Marbles.

NUR. What?

JADEN. You know, the little glass balls.

NUR. God you're ancient.

JADEN. A Batman rucksack.

NUR. Go on.

JADEN. A chess set, Manchester United shirt, camel.

NUR. Camel!?

JADEN. Actually we only borrowed the camel!

NUR. Nothing wrong with borrowing.

JADEN. If you give it back!

> JADEN *spins* NUR *around the room*.
>
> JADEN *and* NUR *are giddy. They pause to get their breath back*.

NUR. I was thinking, maybe we could borrow a couple of paintings from Mustafa's house. Sell 'em. Use the money for daycare.

JADEN. Have you lost your mind!?

NUR. He has hundreds of paintings.

JADEN. If it wasn't for Mustafa we wouldn't be here!

NUR. Daycare means you can get a proper job.

JADEN. I'm the daycare! Aya loves being with me. It's the perfect system!

NUR *walks over to* BABY AYA.

If you wake her now the little gazelle will scream all night.

NUR. Good. (*With accent.*) Hopefully someone will hear us.

JADEN. I wish you wouldn't mutter in English.

NUR. Fucking learn the language then.

*Beat.*

NUR *goes over to the tree, rips off a leaf and begins to chew.*

JADEN. You're chewing.

NUR. You've got eyes.

NUR *and* JADEN *look at each other.*

When you look at Aya, what do you see?

JADEN. … a baby.

NUR. Is that all?

JADEN. Yes.

NUR *chews some more and stares at* JADEN.

*Beat.*

How's college?

NUR. I don't belong there.

JADEN. It's too easy for you?

NUR *shakes her head.*

*Beat.*

NUR. Aya is the best thing that ever happened to me. If I was to lose her, I'd fall into a hole. I can't – I won't let that happen.

If I thought that was going to, if there was someone who I thought might be responsible for that happening, I'd find a sharp thing, like like scissors or just a sharp pencil, and I would do something awful. To their neck. Or their balls. While they slept.

*Beat.*

JADEN. I too would tear apart anyone who hurt Aya. If I couldn't find a weapon... be it a household thingy or piece of stationery – I'd use my teeth.
When you're at college, we talk. To the untrained ear it'll sound like a lot of bleh doh goo glll hmm boo la gll gll da da da da da. But it's something deeper, something special. It transcends life and death.

*Beat.*

NUR. Do you still think about the man?

JADEN. ... yeah.

NUR. I thought his friends would've come. But every night they don't, I think, maybe, we'll be... (okay.)

JADEN *hugs his knees close to his chest.*

(*Gently.*) Jaden.

JADEN. Mm.

NUR. Are you alone?

*Beat.*

JADEN. Always.

NUR. Are you cold?

JADEN. Very.

*Beat.*

NUR. Do the moths still eat your duvet?

JADEN. They do.

*Beat.*

I might have a little chew first.

NUR. Sure.

JADEN *rips off some leaves from the tree and begins to chew.*

When you're ready come to me. Never to her. We have something special. I'm here. She isn't. She's never.

JADEN *and* NUR *begin to touch each other. It is tender.*

BABY AYA *opens her eyes to watch.*

## Seven

BABY AYA. **IT'S A WEDNESDAY. MOM COMES HOME LATE FROM SCHOOL ON A WEDNESDAY. FUUUUUUUUUUUUCK.**

JADEN *is asleep.* BABY AYA *is wide awake.*

Jaden.

JADEN. Mm.

BABY AYA. I'm hungry.

JADEN. Trying to talk aren't you?

BABY AYA. You got a banana or something.

JADEN. Who's my favourite girl?

BABY AYA. For fuck's sake.

JADEN. Who's my favourite girl?

BABY AYA. I could murder some porridge.

JADEN. I had a strange dream about a horse. It had two heads. One could sing like my grandma.

BABA AYA *holds out her arms.*

Don't like the buggy do you?

BABY AYA. I'm not sure what I think about it.

JADEN. Just a few more weeks, I'm saving up, just a few more –

JADEN *looks at the giant tree.*

BABY AYA. Not yet.

JADEN *approaches the tree.*

Don't. The rabbits!

JADEN *reaches for a leaf.*

Shit. (*Sings the first line of 'I Want to Break Free' by Queen.*)

JADEN…. ?

BABY AYA *sings the next line.*

JADEN *picks off a leaf.* BABY AYA *sings to* JADEN *like her life depended on it.*
BABY AYA *sings a verse.*
JADEN *sings a verse.*

Where's Nur?

BABY AYA. She meets with the council on Wednesdays, you know that, search inside your head.

JADEN *pops a leaf into his mouth.*

Spit it out!

JADEN. Tastes worse than Qatal, which is saying something.

BABY AYA. Qatal is harmless. The shit you grow is toxic.

JADEN. I miss chewing the real flower of paradise. Sitting with the boys. Talking politics, football, loss. A time with no agenda. Problems would be solved. Crises averted. And it didn't matter if you were a beggar or a sheik. Whoever loses gold can find it in the jewellery shop but whoever loses their home will not find it anywhere. Maybe I romanticise?

JADEN *stuffs another leaf into his mouth.*

BABY AYA. The rabbits will come – STOP.

JADEN *sings the bridge of 'I Want to Break Free' by Queen.*

GUNSHOT-WOUND RABBIT *enters.*

JADEN. Mr Rabbit.

BABY AYA. Oh fuck.

JADEN. I've always respected your kind. Our political and religious beliefs differ but I've always tolerated you. Please leave my plant alone.

BABY AYA. Spit it out, they'll disappear.

GUNSHOT-WOUND RABBIT *picks off a leaf and chews.*

JADEN. Stop – please.

GUNSHOT-WOUND RABBIT *picks off another leaf.*

Go to Mustafa's garden he has so many plants, I'll leave you an area, praise be to God.

BABY AYA. Get out of your head – feed me!

GUNSHOT-WOUND RABBIT (*looking at* BABY AYA). Is she for sale?

JADEN. No that's, she's not, that's that's, she's my my my my –

GUNSHOT-WOUND RABBIT *puts another leaf into his mouth. Chews and stares at* BABY AYA.

GUNSHOT-WOUND RABBIT. I can pay fifteen hundred pounds.

JADEN. She's a baby!

GUNSHOT-WOUND RABBIT. I know I'm just so fucking horny.

GUNSHOT-WOUND RABBIT *chews and chews.*

There was another girl living here.

JADEN. Only the baby and me live here.

GUNSHOT-WOUND RABBIT. Tell me her name or I'll smash the baby's head against the wall.

*Beat.*

JADEN. Nur.

GUNSHOT-WOUND RABBIT. Nur! That's it. The men wanted her a few years ago but I said let's wait. Children can be tricky to work with.

JADEN. She's still a child.

GUNSHOT-WOUND RABBIT. It's a ticket out of this shithole. She'll get a starter home. A husband. Heck I'll even throw in a honeymoon.

*Beat.*

*JADEN runs to* BABY AYA. *Cuts a tuft of hair sprouting from her helmet. Throws the hair at the* GUNSHOT-WOUND RABBIT, *who retreats.*

(*Like Schwarzenegger.*) *I'll be back.*

GUNSHOT-WOUND RABBIT *exits.*
JADEN *runs to the tap and drinks.*
BABY AYA *pants for liquid.*

JADEN. Did you see my darling? Your hair saved us! They can't cope with striking hair. It sends them into a frenzy. They're okay with my grey bits of straw… but a woman's hair… it's like the sun. It makes them melt.

BABY AYA. Gimme WATER!

JADEN. It's four-thirty you must be starving!

BABY AYA. (YOU THINK!?)

*JADEN runs to the fridge. Takes out some blackberries.*
BABY AYA *eats blackberries. Makes a real mess on her face.*

*JADEN stuffs leaves into his mouth and stares at* BABY AYA.

JADEN. I promised your grandpa I'd look after Nur. I'm not sure I'm doing a good job. I wonder if she'd… you'd… be better off without (me)

BABY AYA *opens her mouth very wide.*
JADEN *suddenly remembers to give* BABY AYA *her water bottle. She slowly manipulates it towards her mouth in the way ten-month-old babies do.*

JADEN. Is Yusrah going to visit today?

BABY AYA. You're insane. Someone should tranquilise you.

**Eight**

BABY AYA *is in a cot!*
NUR *is blindfolded and being led by* JADEN *towards the cot.*

NUR. Is this going to be like the time when you made me eat snake?

JADEN. Nearly there.

JADEN *takes of* NUR*'s blindfold.*

NUR. Whoa. Where d'ya find it?

JADEN. Skip at the end of the road was full of wood. Got a hammer and some nails and the rest is history!

NUR. I'm impressed. Hey Aya, aren't you lucky to have someone who can make things.

BABY AYA. I'm the luckiest girl in the world.

NUR. Now you can have tummy time.

BABY AYA. What's tummy time?

NUR. It's when you lie on your front.

BABY AYA. Oh I've done that before.

JADEN. Sometimes I think you two are talking to each other.

BABY AYA. We are you dozy pervert.

JADEN. She looks happy doesn't she? Maybe she knows she'll never have to sleep in the buggy again.

BABY AYA. Feel free to burn it.

JADEN. Now we'll only need it for walks in the park and when we go to Mustafa's!

BABY AYA. Not for long though...

BABY AYA *uses the cot to life herself up so she is standing.*

NUR. Oh yessss Aya!

JADEN. Who's a clever girl!?

BABY AYA. Plenty more where that came from.

BABY AYA *hoists her feet off the ground as if she's an Olympian gymnast.* NUR *and* JADEN *applaud.*

*The cot collapses.*

NUR. / Aya!

JADEN. OH / GOD!

NUR. Are you / okay?

BABY AYA. What happened? Am I dead?

NUR. No you're / not

JADEN. Is she / okay?

BABY AYA. I don't know.

NUR. I think she's alright.

JADEN. She's not hurt is she?

NUR. No she's – were you chewing?

BABY AYA. Mum I wanna go back in the buggy.

NUR. Were you chewing when you made this?

JADEN *shakes his head.*

Show me your eyes show me your eyes!

BABY AYA. Mum, put me in the –

NUR. You're eyes are red, they're red

JADEN. I'm not chewing, I've cut down, I promise.

NUR. How many times have we heard that!?

JADEN. I love you girls, I love you too much.

BABY AYA. PUT ME IN THE FUCKING BUGGY!

NUR. SHUT UP AYA!

JADEN. Nur!?
    Mummy doesn't mean to shout...

    JADEN *goes to get the buggy.*

NUR. What are you doing?

JADEN. Putting her in the buggy / while I fix

NUR. Look at her head! How can you put her in the buggy!?

JADEN. She has a helmet.

NUR. It's not working.

BABY AYA. Isn't it!?

JADEN. The doctor said it could take three months.

NUR. I can't do this.
    We should call...

JADEN. Don't talk like a maniac.

    NUR *takes out her phone.*

NUR. **NUR COULD MAKE A PHONE CALL. A PHONE
CALL THAT COULD CHANGE THE DESTINY OF
THIS FAMILY.**

JADEN. With your brains and my brawn we're unstoppable.

NUR. I don't think so.

JADEN. We're a team!

BABY AYA. I'm shitting.

NUR. The brains and brawn aren't enough.

JADEN. Where's your optimism gone?

BABY AYA. I've shat myself.

JADEN. You used to be smiley. Your eyes would glint with mischief. You would tease me, play pranks. Now you are serious. And there are lines on your face.

*Beat.*

NUR. I do smile.

BABY AYA. Mum change me.

NUR. Aya deserves more.

JADEN. More of what?

BABY AYA. Change me.

NUR. Everything.

JADEN. Aya needs love, food, and somewhere to sleep. We've got the first two.

NUR. I'm not sure.

JADEN. What are you saying?

NUR. Aya needs more than just somewhere to sleep.

BABY AYA. It's cool I can sit in it for a bit.

NUR. Jaden we –

JADEN. If speech is of silver, silence is golden.

JADEN *begins to rebuild the cot.*

NUR. Maybe they can help us.

JADEN. They'd take her away.

NUR. Maybe she needs to be taken away.

BABY AYA. I'M COVERED IN SHIT, I THOUGHT I COULD HANDLE IT BUT I CAN'T!

NUR. Change her.

JADEN *begins to change* BABY AYA.

JADEN. She's clean.
And dry.
Little gazelle what are you screaming about?

NUR *begins to scroll through her phone.*

BABY AYA. Mum, don't call.

NUR *starts to dial.*
JADEN *grabs the phone and throws it at the back wall. Smash!*

NUR. We're at the bottom of the ocean. I can't see a thing. No danger, no future, no nothing. How do we (live)?

BABY AYA. Mum hold me.

NUR....

BABY AYA (*softly*). Hold me.

NUR. I... I... (can't)

BABY AYA. Then let me hold you.

NUR. In a second.
Jaden.
Look at me.

JADEN. What?

NUR. There's like a space in my chest.

BABY AYA. Mum breathe!

NUR. A space in my chest, and then the heat comes, so much heat, and though it burns it feels so good.

JADEN. Are you having a panic attack?

NUR. Don't you feel the space? And then the heat?

JADEN. !?

NUR (*near tears*). You must feel it!?

JADEN. How is the college council?

NUR. Oh my God.

JADEN. Going well?

NUR. You're changing the subject.

JADEN. I'm not going to talk nonsense about space and heat! How is the council?

NUR. I'm not...

JADEN. You're not what?

NUR. I'm not in the college council.

JADEN. But they asked you, they were so impressed with how you'd managed with Aya and –

NUR. I quit college two weeks ago.

JADEN. What!?

NUR. I quit college two weeks ago.

JADEN....

Where have you been going every day!?

NUR. Looking for work. Or sometimes I'm here *all day*.

JADEN. We left so you could go to school.

NUR. We didn't have a choice!

JADEN. Course we had a – you don't think Yus, me, your parents didn't agonise for months –

NUR. Yusrah never wanted to come. You made her. And now... a crab is probably scuttling through her eye socket.

*A very, very tense beat.*

BABY AYA. Group hug?
  Orgy?

  NUR *tears a leaf off the giant tree and offers it to* JADEN.

  *Beat.*
  JADEN *leaves the room.*
  BABY AYA *crawls across the filthy floor towards the buggy.*
  *Lifts herself up triumphantly.*

  Mum put your hands on the buggy, push us out of the room.
  Don't look back or you'll turn to salt.

NUR. We're a family, we're a team so we / stick (together)

BABY AYA. Take off my helmet.

NUR. We only do that during bathtime.

BABY AYA. Take it off!

  NUR *takes off the helmet.*

  Does that look like teamwork?

NUR. Your hair!?

BABY AYA. Jaden, he. He. He... has...
  (No.)
  I've been pulling it out.

NUR. Don't you want your hair to grow long and pretty?

BABY AYA. Jaden says I look better short.

NUR. Does he.

  NUR *picks up the smashed phone. It's still working.*

BABY AYA. Jaden loves your hair the most he always goes on
  about how beautiful you are ALWAYS so don't worry about
  me, I'm no threat, I'm just like a cuddly toy.

NUR....
  They'll move you into a room with a new cot. A cot that
  doesn't break. You'll never be cold. You'll never be thirsty or
  hungry. And you'll have a new mum. A mum that is... kinder.

BABY AYA. Mum, I don't fucking know any other mums. I don't know any other babies. It's a shame we don't get a choice day one, but here we are... intertwined.

My voice is hoarse and my skin is leathery and my lungs are battered. My joints are beginning to stiffen. My eyes are learning to not see. My ears are learning to not hear. I know I'm a chatterbox but if you're patient with me, I'll soon be mute. So in a short while, I'll be no trouble, no bother at all. You'll barely know I exist.

I've no idea how long a life should be.
But while I'm still around,
I'd like to spend the time with you.

**Nine**

*The house lights snap on.*

BABY AYA *is alone in her buggy. Unlike normal, she is strapped in.*

BABY AYA. **HAS BABY AYA BEEN LEFT FOR DEAD IN THIS SHITTY ROOM THAT TIME FORGOT? IF ONLY SHE HAD A FULL SET OF TEETH, SHE COULD CHEW HER WAY TO FREEDOM. AS DAY TURNS TO NIGHT, AYA GETS TO THINKING. ABOUT WHO DAD MIGHT BE. ABOUT WHY MOM WON'T JUST RESCUE HER.**

*We're back in the prologue scene.* BABY AYA *watches... but of course she wasn't there.*

NUR, *aged sixteen, runs into the room. Breathes. Smiles at us. Seems she's lost her pursuer.*

*Another* MAN *enters, different to the one in the prologue.* NUR *collapses by the back wall, exhausted, whimpering. The* MAN *lights a cigarette. Keeps his eyes focused on* NUR.

*Unseen by the other two,* JADEN *opens the wardrobe door
from where he's been hiding. He silently bends a wire coat
hanger out of shape.*
*We urge him with every fibre in our body to intervene.*

*The* MAN *stubs out his cigarette. Walks towards* NUR.
*Before he can touch* NUR, JADEN *comes up behind the*
MAN *and starts strangling him with the coat hanger.*

*The struggle pushes* JADEN *and the* MAN *behind the
wardrobe.*

*All we can see are some legs kicking.*
*And then the legs come to a stop.*

JADEN *walks to the back wall and sits next to* NUR.
NUR *leans her head on* JADEN'*s shoulder.*

*Their breath falls into sync.*

## Ten

BABY AYA *is in her buggy. There's a love bite on her neck.*
JADEN *is scattering hair around the room, creating a
perimeter fence.*

JADEN. Too long they've been winning. Not any more.

BABY AYA. Is that Mum's hair?

> JADEN *looks at the tree, salivating. He's going cold turkey.*

JADEN. If Yus wants to come, she'll come.

BABY AYA. What have you done to Mum?

JADEN. More and more you look like her. You have the same mouth. A sensuous mouth. When she was thinking she'd purse her lips.

Go on. Purse your lips.

*Beat.*

Yus.

BABY AYA. I'm Aya.

JADEN. Look. (*Points to the broken cot.*) It's like the empty hut.

BABY AYA. You need psychiatric help.

JADEN. We'd meet at 11 p.m., after your dad fell asleep.

BABY AYA. You've got a poorly mind.

JADEN. I'll bring lamb mandi, kidbe, okra.

BABY AYA. Right we're just having two conversations now.

JADEN. You'd bring speakers. I'd want Kadim but you'd always insist on Queen.

You knew all the words. (*Sings the first two lines of the second verse of 'I Want to Break Free' by Queen.*) – Yus.

I'm not sure if I'm making this up.

BABY AYA....

JADEN. Tell me it's true.

BABY AYA. I'm Aya.

JADEN. The best times is when we chewed together.

JADEN *tears off a leaf and puts in* BABY AYA*'s mouth.*

BABY AYA *screams.*

What have you done with Yusrah?

BABY AYA....?

JADEN. Is she inside you?

BABY AYA....

JADEN. Are you a djinn!?

BABY AYA. Don't come at me with that old country crap.

JADEN. Have you possessed her!?

    JADEN *gets the tin opener.*

BABY AYA. Mum!

JADEN. Release her.

BABY AYA. FUCK! MUM!

JADEN. Or I'll cut her out.

    BABY AYA *purses her lips.*

    Yusrah.

BABY AYA. Uh-huh.

JADEN. You came back.

BABY AYA. Yeah.

JADEN. OH YUSRAH!

BABY AYA. SURPRISE. (*Shakes her hands like jazz hands.*)

JADEN. Look – the hut.

BABY AYA. Yes, the hut.

JADEN. Remember our nights.

    BABY AYA *nods.*

    You'd hold my zub with both hands despite it not being big
    enough for both hands.

    BABY AYA *frowns.*

    Maybe you did it to make me feel powerful?

    BABY AYA *shrugs.*

    You've forgotten?

    BABY AYA *nods.*

Are you trying to forget?

BABY AYA *shakes her head.*

The men said we'd only be in the lorry for three hours…
three hours…

BABY AYA. It's okay. *Dad.*

JADEN. Can you hold him like you used to?

*Beat.*

BABY AYA. Alright.

JADEN *unzips his flies. Walks towards* BABY AYA.

*At the last possible moment,* JADEN *sees* BABY AYA *and
not Yusrah. A gasp. Backs off to the other side of the room.*

JADEN. Oh little gazelle.

BABY AYA. Don't cry, don't cry, Jaden.

GUNSHOT-WOUND RABBIT *and* BURNT-FUR RABBIT
*enter the room. Casually lollop over the circle of hair. They
wear sunglasses. They might also rub factor-fifty sun cream
into their fur so they are totally unfazed by the hair.*

*The* RABBITS *look at* BABY AYA.

GUNSHOT-WOUND RABBIT *raps a verse from 'Fuck You'
by Dr Dre.*
BURNT-FUR RABBIT *joins in on the chorus.*

*The* RABBITS *approach* BABY AYA. *They take off her
helmet. Toss it on the other side of the room.*

AHHHHH KEEP IT ON KEEP IT ON!

JADEN. Stop stop take your hands off her – take, take –

JADEN *steps inside the wardrobe.*

*Beat.*

*The* RABBITS *pile inside the wardrobe. The doors are
closed. There are screams and thumps from inside.*

BABY AYA. Jaden there's hair on my shoulders you can have that!

BABY AYA *waits for a response.*

There's still a couple of clumps on my head!

*The screams from the wardrobe transform into sounds of war.*
BABY AYA *pulls open her Babygro.*

Yusrah is here! Come for Yusrah!

*The war noises crescendo.*

BABY AYA *sings the second verse of 'I Want to Break Free' by Queen.*

BABY AYA's *song can't compete with the war sounds.*

*EXPLOSION SOUNDS! And then everything goes silent.*

NUR *enters. Her hair is shorter.*

Oh Mum you're alive!

NUR. I can see your skin.

BABY AYA. When did you get all prudish?

NUR. It's not prud– it's, you can't, you can't just parade around like that.

BABY AYA. Why? There aren't any men here.

BABY AYA *winks at a man in the audience.*

NUR *buttons up* BABY AYA's *Babygro.*

NUR. What's your helmet doing on the other side of the room?

BABY AYA....

NUR *straps the helmet back onto* BABY AYA's *head.*

When a bad thing happens, does a part of you, feel, responsible?

NUR. (Yes!) Whatever happened, you'd never be, no part of you would be, responsible.

BABY AYA. Is my helmet on correctly?

NUR. Yeah.

BABY AYA. Has the buggy flattened the back of my head forever?

NUR. Your head is still soft, all babies have soft – so it can change / back

BABY AYA. I don't mind the helmet now. It keeps me together.

NUR. It's coming off. The doctor, she said a few more weeks. And then you will have a head that's round like a ball. Or maybe an egg. You came out of me so quickly your head was egg-shaped. Anyway, it's going to return to its natural (shape) and no part of you is responsible for – that's the buggy's fault and that's our (fault)
On Friday I get paid. Next week you'll have a new cot. Not one from a skip. But from Argos.

BABY AYA. Wow.

NUR *hugs* BABY AYA.

Jaden scratches me.

BABY AYA *lets out a breath. She's been waiting her entire life to say this.*

NUR. ...

BABY AYA. He doesn't mean to scratch. It's just he chews and wants a cuddle.

NUR. He cuddles you?

BABY AYA. Are you trying to go deaf too?

NUR. He doesn't cuddle...

*Beat.*

BABY AYA. I s'pose we can share the cuddles. Sharing is caring.

NUR. So you *like* the cuddles.

BABY AYA.... I'm not sure.

NUR. I bet you love them.

BABY AYA.... sometimes.

> NUR *puts her head in her hands*.

> Have I done something wrong?

> NUR *shakes her head*.

> They make him happy.

NUR (*softly*). That's good.

> BABY AYA *smiles, pleased with herself.*
> *Her smile fades*.

BABY AYA. But then the bunnies come.

NUR. Bunnies?

BABY AYA. The buck-tooth perverts.

NUR. Aya you're confused. The bunnies go to Mustafa's garden. They dig up his flowerbeds.

BABY AYA. They come here.

NUR. No they don't – and the scratches aren't from – you scratch yourself remember?

BABY AYA. Do I?

NUR. You do. But that's okay. All babies scratch themselves.

BABY AYA....

NUR. And you pull your hair out. You've got to stop that too. Not exactly a good look. Scratched and bald.

BABY AYA. Some men like it.

> *Beat*.

NUR. Are you tired?

BABY AYA. I've been asleep all day.

NUR. You look tired.

BABY AYA. I feel quite awake.

NUR. Your eyelids are drooping over.

BABY AYA. Mum you're being really strange.

NUR. I'm just looking out for you. I don't want you to get sick cos you got tired. Let me feel your head. You're hot.

BABY AYA. I'm freezing!

NUR. Then you definitely have a temperature!

BABY AYA. Really!?

NUR. You're burning up.

BABY AYA. Am I!?

NUR. There's nothing to worry about.

BABY AYA. Will I be okay?

NUR. Yes you just need to sleep it off.

BABY AYA. Okay I'll try.

NUR. With both eyes closed. With both ears closed.

BABY AYA. Will I die?

NUR. Not if you sleep. Close your eyes now. You'll feel better in the morning.

BABY AYA. Sing to me.

NUR *sings 'Yalla Tnam'.*

BABY AYA *falls asleep.*

NUR *gets a pillow and approaches* BABY AYA.

NUR *tosses away the pillow. Slumps to the floor.*

JADEN *steps out of the wardrobe. He might be bleeding.*

NUR. How are the rabbits?

JADEN....?

NUR. That dig up Mustafa's garden.

JADEN. Don't be ridiculous, there aren't any rabbits in
    Knightsbridge.

NUR. You cut off our hair!

JADEN. I didn't.

NUR. Do you forget or do you excuse?

JADEN. You've lost me Nur.

NUR. I think you're quite sick.

JADEN. !?

NUR. You need a doctor.

JADEN. I feel fine.

NUR. Not for your body – for your mind.

JADEN. I don't need a doctor.

NUR. You've done things you would not do back home.

    NUR *takes out an axe*.

    It's time to cut down the / tree

JADEN. Don't you dare.

NUR. It makes you see stuff that isn't real.

JADEN. When I chew Yusrah visits.

NUR. Only in your head!
    Cut down the tree. Cut it down before you properly hurt us.

JADEN. I would never hurt you...

    NUR *hands* JADEN *the axe*.

NUR. I'll get you real leaves. Natural, pure stuff.

JADEN *tosses the axe away.*
*Distant sounds of war.*

BABY AYA. Morning soldier.

*The war sounds increase.*

JADEN. Shit.

BABY AYA. **THIS ROOM AIN'T BIG ENOUGH FOR THE THREE OF US.**

JADEN. They're coming.

NUR. Who?

JADEN. The men dressed as bunnies.

BABY AYA. Told you.

NUR. There are no men dressed as bunnies!

JADEN. You both need to leave now.

NUR. Calm down.

JADEN. You don't understand the danger.

NUR. What danger!?

JADEN. They want Aya, they want you –

BURNT-FUR RABBIT *lollops in with an AK-47.*

NUR. OH FUCK.

NUR *can see the* RABBIT*!*
GUNSHOT-WOUND RABBIT *lollops in with a bazooka.*

JADEN. I beg you leave my family in peace.

BABY AYA. Motherfucker's talking to bunnies again.

BURNT-FUR RABBIT *(about* NUR*).* She looks like the baby.

JADEN. It's called genes you thugs!

BURNT-FUR RABBIT. Then give us her genes.

NUR. This isn't real.

GUNSHOT-WOUND RABBIT. Give us her tongue.

JADEN. What?

GUNSHOT-WOUND RABBIT. Cut out her tongue.

NUR. It's just you me and Aya.

BURNT-FUR RABBIT. A woman needs a mouth not a tongue.

JADEN. You're barbarians!

GUNSHOT-WOUND RABBIT. We only want her tongue.

BURNT-FUR RABBIT. I'd like her ears.

NUR. Oh my God oh / my God.

GUNSHOT-WOUND RABBIT. No her ears would be barbaric.
    Just cut out her tongue and we'll be offsky.

JADEN. You're not having any of her.

GUNSHOT-WOUND RABBIT. Give us her tongue or we'll
    have all of her at the same time.

BURNT-FUR RABBIT. And eat the baby we're fucking starving.

    JADEN *is on his knees.*

JADEN. Don't take the girls!

    *Beat.*

GUNSHOT-WOUND RABBIT. We'll leave you with one.
    Let's take Nur.

BURNT-FUR RABBIT. I'd prefer the old baby.

GUNSHOT-WOUND RABBIT. Fine. Toss for it.

    GUNSHOT-WOUND RABBIT *takes out a gold coin.*
    *As both* RABBITS *look at the coin,* JADEN *runs to* BURNT-
    FUR RABBIT *and grabs the AK-47. He aims for the*
    RABBITS *but sprays bullets around the room. Everyone*
    *runs for cover.*
    *Miraculously, at the end of the round,* JADEN *has missed*
    *everyone.*

JADEN (*still pointing the gun at the rabbits*). You're not taking either of them. You'll have to shoot me first.

GUNSHOT-WOUND RABBIT *shrugs. Fires his bazooka at* JADEN. JADEN *flies across the room.*

*The* RABBITS *turn their attention to* NUR *and* BABY AYA.
*The* RABBITS *comb their hair.*
*Eat a Smint or spray breath-freshener.*
*Apply aftershave to face and crotch.*
*They're like nervous adolescent virgins.*

NUR *darts to pick up the axe and starts to hack at the tree.*
*The tree crashes to the floor.*
*The* RABBITS *disappear.*

JADEN *slowly sits himself up.*

NUR. Aya and I are going to the park. When we come back the whole tree must be gone. No leaves no seeds no nothing.
If you can't throw it out, then you must take it with you.
I've started praying again. And I'm praying you throw it out.

JADEN. Don't leave.

NUR. We'll be back in an hour.

(*To* JADEN.) Make a decision. Make the right decision.
Fuck,
I love (you).

NUR *goes to push the buggy towards the exit.*

BABY AYA. No Mum. It won't just stop when the tree goes.
We need to leave. Or we need to put him down. Actually yeah. Use the axe.

*Beat.*

NUR *pushes the buggy towards the exit.*
BABY AYA *jumps out of the buggy and stands unsteady but blocking its path.*

In the park, around the back of the caff, there's a cardboard box and a sleeping bag. It's not a new sleeping bag, it's second hand you can tell by the smell. But it's currently unoccupied. I think it's a good place to set up home. Get my foot on the ladder. It's quite cosy, and although open to the elements being outdoors and all – it is quiet. I could do with… you see… I'm sick to the death of both of you.

NUR. Aya.

BABY AYA. This room ain't big enough for the three of us.

NUR. What if I dropped you at at the hospital?

BABY AYA. I'm a park girl me.

NUR. The park is for the swings. It isn't somewhere to live.

BABY AYA. Disagree. But then, you've never had an eye for potential.

NUR. There are people that can help us.

BABY AYA (*shakes head*). Best not to rely on the state.
I'm pretty good at walking now, I'll make my own way.
(*To* NUR.) Visit me when you can.

    BABY AYA *totters out*.

NUR. Get in the buggy.

BABY AYA. No you're alright.

NUR. Get in the buggy!

BABY AYA. Can I take some nappies for the road?

NUR. Aya. The buggy. Now!

    NUR *sings a line from 'Bound 2' by Kanye West*.
    BABY AYA *sings a line from 'Bound 2' by Kanye West*.

**Eleven**

*The tree has gone. The buggy is empty.*

JADEN. Economics economics, wonderful.
    You're taking over.

NUR. Yeah.

JADEN. In a few years a job in in in a bank?

NUR. Maybe.

JADEN. There's no maybes, no maybes any more only
    definitelys. All our uncertainty, all that we can forget, we can
    wipe all that greyness and unknowingness from our lives
    because now we have a future that is clear. I can see the path.
    There is no Japanese knotweed hijacking our route. It is a
    clear gravel path.
    Twister?

    JADEN *gets out the Twister board. They play in silence for a*
    *while.*

    NUR *walks away.*

    What's up?

NUR. Nothing.

JADEN. Nur?

NUR....

JADEN. Talk to me.

NUR. Stop.

JADEN. Nur.

    *Beat.*

    Smile.

Smile like you used to.
Talk in that zigzag way.
When you were younger you were like a firework.

*Beat.*

Nur.

*Beat.*

Darling.

*Beat.*

My love please. I can't stand it when you're silent.

*Beat.*

I forget how to be with you. Nur say something. Come back
I'm begging, Nur, I can't feel my feet I can't feel my stomach
fingers I'm evaporating I'm disappearing please say something
or at least hold me please Nur please just hold me or tell me
speak English teach me the words teach me anything just talk
say speak – I'm not I'm not I don't think I'm here my feet
aren't on the ground I have no roots where am SPEAK – this is
cruel this is torture you fucking, oh my Nur, I can't carry on
unless you speak touch just something a whisper a breath I
don't want to be alone don't leave me alone –

NUR *walks towards* JADEN *and holds his hand.*
JADEN*'s jagged breaths begin to calm.*

It's better now, it's how it was, we know how to do *this*.
We're better as a two.

NUR *looks at the empty buggy.*

*Manages to pull herself away from looking at the buggy.*
*Looks at us.*

NUR. **The future.**
   **Aya is four years old. It's her first day of school. She
   picks up conkers on the way.**

JADEN. **Aya is seven years old. She gets caught smoking at
   the bus stop.**

NUR. **Aya is eleven years old. She's so advanced she does her GSCEs early.**

JADEN. **Aya is nineteen and volunteers in a soup kitchen.**

NUR. **Aya is twenty-four and ballroom dances on a Tuesday. She meets a girl called Lucy.**

JADEN. **Aya is twenty-five. She's courting a nice boy from a good family. He's a doctor, accountant or lawyer.**

NUR. **Aya is twenty-nine and in a moment of existential angst, slaps a priest.**

JADEN. **Aya is thirty-two and –**

NUR. **Aya is thirty-eight**

JADEN. **Forty-one**

NUR. **Forty-five**

JADEN. **Fifty-six**

NUR. **Seventy-two**

JADEN. **Aya is older.**

NUR. **Aya is. Old.**

> NUR *and* JADEN *smile at the audience.*
>
> *End.*

# THE MIKVAH PROJECT

*The Mikvah Project* was first performed at The Yard, London, on 17 February 2015. The cast was as follows:

EITAN                              Oliver Coopersmith
AVI                                Jonah Russell

*Director*                         Jay Miller
*Designer*                         Cecile Tremolieres
*Lighting and Video Designer*      Josh Pharo
*Sound Designer*                   Josh Grigg
*Composer*                         Ezra Burke

## Acknowledgements

I'd like to thank Jay Miller for going on a journey with me to develop this play. A number of artists were involved in pre-production workshops; Paul Virides, Emily Kempson, Leon Waltz, Ezra Burke, Josh Miles, Patrick Walshe McBride, Tom Lincoln, Matthew Tennyson, Elliot Levy. Their contributions were invaluable.

Lastly, to Jonah and Oli, who made the experience both funnier and more moving than I could ever imagine.

**Characters**

EITAN, *seventeen years old*
AVI, *thirty-five years old*

**Place**

A space somewhere between a Mikvah and a theatre.

A Mikvah is a large pool of water in which Jews immerse.

Scenes outside of the Mikvah should be played directly to the audience.

**Time**

Now.

**Notes on the Text**

... indicates an unspoken throught or a character struggling to articulate a thought.

Spaces between lines indicate beats and pauses.

## ACT ONE

### Scene One

*A large pool of water dominates the space.*

EITAN *enters.*

EITAN (*to audience*). Hello.
Welcome to [*insert name of theatre in which the play is being performed*].
This is a Mikvah. My friend and I built it.
A Mikvah is a gathering of spring water.
We had to dig a really deep hole before we found water.
Then, we inserted a pipe,
To suck up the required nine hundred litres.
Now,
this bad boy,
is KOSHER.
My friend is directly below us checking the filtration system.
Can you hear him?
Listen.
There he goes, clinky clank with his spanner.
Every night there's checks to be done. We have a rota.

You'll love my friend. He's got insane facial hair. I think people call it designer stubble. Imagine George Clooney, five inches shorter, two stone heavier and with a bulbus nose, that's my friend.

AVI *enters.*

AVI (*to audience*). Hello.

EITAN. Is it warm down there tonight?

AVI. Yep.

EITAN. Must be a rush being underground with yer toolbox bet you feel like a man?

AVI. We should get started.

EITAN. Introduce yourself then.

AVI. Avi is married to Leyla. Happily married for seven years. He works as a director of communications for a human-rights charity.
Baruch HaShem life is good.

EITAN. They don't have any children.

AVI. Not yet, we're taking things slow.

EITAN. Eitan is a seventeen-year-old Jew. He got three thousand, four hundred and twenty pounds for his bar mitzvah and has yet to spend a penny.

AVI. That image doesn't help our reputation.

EITAN. I think I'm going to invest it in shares.

AVI. Take off your clothes.

EITAN. Steady on.

AVI. Or leave.
We need to immerse.

EITAN. Men don't go to the Mikvahs. Unless they're hassids or fanatics, or fanatical hassids.

AVI. I go to the Mikvah. Do I look like a hassid?

EITAN. Why you here?

AVI. … to be spiritually cleansed.

EITAN. This Mikvah is in Stamford Hill.

AVI. This Mikvah is in Hampstead Garden Suburb.

EITAN. Our story would go down a treat in Stamford Hill.

AVI. They'd stone you.

EITAN. And you!

AVI. This Mikvah is in Hampstead Garden Suburb.

EITAN. It's very quiet, in fact it's just the two of us.

AVI. On a Friday.

EITAN. After school.

AVI. But before the Shabbat rush hour.

EITAN. Avi undresses. He hangs his clothes on the little hooks.

AVI. He also removes his kippah and his tzisit.

EITAN. It's long to wear those for our story, what with the
    water

AVI. So just imagine.

EITAN. We're those type of Jews

AVI. Postmodern Orthodox!

EITAN. The Mikvah changing rooms are nasty.
    Like Neasden Leisure Centre.

AVI. Neasden doesn't have a leisure centre.

EITAN. But if it did, it would look like this.

AVI. Take off your clothes.

EITAN. It's very cold.
    Anyway, I'm not feeling too – (*Says some Hebrew which
    translates as 'immerse and be pure'.*)

AVI. Show-off.

EITAN. 'Immerse and be pure!'

AVI. Avi walks to the showers.
    Checks the temperature.
    Goes under
    And scrubs.


EITAN. Look at his muscles tense relax tense relax tense tense
    tense – you looking to scrub off your skin!?

AVI. Gotta be clean before immersion.

Avi lathers up his shoulders chest stomach groin thigh buttoc–

EITAN *leaves*.

Strange boy.

Avi turns off the shower. Stands by the edge of the Mikvah.

And prays to his balls.

Zarach Zarach Zarach.

### Scene Two

EITAN. Eitan is in synagogue for Shabbat. His younger brother is on the choir. His elder brother prays furiously. Look at him go. Mentalist. His dad is snoozing – shirt bursting at the buttons as his tummy spills out. Rabbi Ovadiah starts his sermon. HaShem creates the world. His best achievement is man, but man alone is imperfect, so a woman is made from his rib. Together. They are perfect.

I look through the mechitza at the women's gallery. Not much going on. Try to eye-fuck my butters second cousin. But she's looking at somebody else. Where does one buy an assault rifle?

AVI *enters*.

I see Avi.

Shaking hands.

Then he kisses his dad.

Tells Danny Altros a joke.

Squeezes Doctor Orenski.

Walks up to the Bimah.

And sings.

AVI (*singing*). *Ein keloheinu, ein kadoneinu, ein kemalkeinu, ein kemosheinu.*

*Mi keloheinu, mi kadoneinu, mi kemalkeinu, mi kemosheinu.*

EITAN. Shabbat Shalom.

AVI. Shabbat Shalom.

AVI *undresses and gets into the Mikvah.*

EITAN. That evening, whilst I sleep, something happens.
I wake up.
Wet.

**Scene Three**

AVI *is immersing in the Mikvah.*

EITAN *interrupts.*

EITAN. How many times are you supposed to go under?

AVI. Three.

EITAN. Why three?

AVI. Mikvah is mentioned three times in the Torah.

EITAN. So that's your three done.

AVI. I do nine.

EITAN. What?

AVI. Have you come to immerse?

EITAN. Why nine?

AVI. By the time you've had a shower, I'll be out, so go on.

EITAN. I like your layning. When you sing, it's smooth,
effortless, like the note just comes out pure, it's not like you
need to blast it out like musicals, do you watch, have you
seen in musicals how they, do you know what I'm talking
about?

AVI *looks at* EITAN.

It's proper cringe. You see these people bending their backs
and their faces go purple and constipated. They're basically
shouting.
But with you, it's different, it's a vibe.
What's your top note?

AVI. B-flat.

EITAN. Rate that.

AVI *gets out of the Mikvah and begins to dress.*

I've resigned from the choir.

AVI. I heard you got kicked out.

EITAN. A few weeks ago I had the Tehilah solo and you know
you only get four notes, ah, ah, ah, well I really fucked –
sorry – my voice nosedived on the final 'ah' so it ended very
badly but Philip shouldn't have

AVI. Defacing the song sheets eh?

EITAN. Hardly – I was rewriting, I was composing!
Where were you that week?

AVI. In the Lake District.

EITAN. Bet there ain't any synagogues up there.
What did you do on Shabbas? Shoot pheasants?

AVI. Shouldn't you go change and shower?

EITAN. What's the rush?

AVI. I just thought you may need to get somewhere.

EITAN. This isn't a problem is it – us talking?

Did you shoot anything then?

AVI. Er, no.

EITAN. What did you do?

AVI. We went for long walks. Hung out in the hotel.

EITAN. Go on sing a B-flat.

AVI. What?

EITAN. Sing a B-flat.

AVI. Sorry?

EITAN. Nothing wrong with singing in a Mikvah is there?

AVI. Don't be silly.

> EITAN *looks at* AVI.

> AVI *sings a B-flat*.

EITAN. Rate that.

AVI. Thanks.
You're too old to sing the Tehilah solo.

EITAN. Exactly. But there are no kids who can do it.

AVI. Your brother's got a decent treble.

EITAN. Are you mad!? The only reason Dovid is on the choir is because he's got chubby cheeks. The congregation think: 'sweet boy'. Nobody actually wants him to sing.

> EITAN *attempts a high note for himself*.

How long till my voice breaks properly?

AVI. It should stop quivering in the next year or two.

EITAN. Do you reckon I'll end up as a tenor or a bass?

AVI. Can't say.

EITAN. High baritone. I'd be down for that.
(*Beat*.)
My older brother told me a riddle.

AVI. Avi turns to exit.

EITAN. If I get the answer, he'll gimme his ID.

AVI. Sorry must dash

EITAN. Hear me out, it'll take two secs.
Eitan launches into a riddle involving nine fat women and a set of weighing scales.

AVI. You tried that riddle with your mum?

EITAN. She's shit at riddles.

AVI. That's besides the point. It's a little misogynistic.

EITAN. What's misogynistic?

AVI. I must leave.

EITAN. Let's work it out together.

AVI. Ask your dad.

EITAN. He sweats when I talk.

AVI *turns around*.

AVI. This riddle.

EITAN. Yes!

AVI. I'm substituting women for something more palatable. Tennis balls.

EITAN. If that makes you feel better.

AVI. So there are nine tennis balls, yes?

EITAN. And one is heavier than the other eight.

AVI. To work out which is heaviest, I have weighing scales?

EITAN. Which you can only use twice.

AVI. So nine balls.
One is heavier than the other eight.
And I can only use the scales twice...

AVI*'s face lights up*.

**Scene Four**

*Music.*

EITAN *is in a club.*

*Sees a girl.*

AVI. Avi is having Shabbat dinner with Leyla.
  They told their parents they'd like to do it alone this week.
  For starters, pumpkin soup.
  Leyla tells Avi about a harrowing work case involving a
  negligent mother and a bruised baby but then lightens the
  mood with gossip about her promiscuous colleague.
  After the soup, they tuck into chicken, rice and okra.
  Avi begins to relay his unusual Mikvah encounter with Eitan
  but then stops.
  Instead he talks about an unsuccessful meeting with a major
  donor who told him he had lost total faith in Avi and the
  whole charity.
  Dessert is apple and pear crumble! Leyla is an amazing
  cook.
  Avi makes a pot of tea with fresh mint picked from the
  garden!
  At this point they have their weekly argument about Gaza.
  After much screaming they both arrive at exactly the same
  point.
  Once the tea is finished…
  Shall we go upstairs?
  The love-making is forceful.
  We complete.
  Leyla runs a bath.
  Avi talks to God about sperm.

**Scene Five**

EITAN *undresses and enters into the water.*

AVI *enters and watches* EITAN, *who is playing in the water unawares.*

AVI. You're not really immersing.

EITAN. Nah just sort of floating…

AVI *undresses.*

AVI. Did you mention the riddle to your mum?

EITAN. Nah. I went clubbing.

AVI. Aren't you a bit young for that?

EITAN. That was why I needed the ID.

AVI. Oh right.

EITAN. Got wasted. Met a girl. Lipsed her.

AVI. Lipsed her?

EITAN. Believe bruv.

AVI. Can we speak 'English'?

EITAN. Bruv is English.
    Racist.

*They laugh.* AVI *joins* EITAN *in the Mikvah. They immerse. After a while their rhythms become similar.*

Eitan has an erection in the Mikvah.
There are options.
Run.
Ignore.
Apologise?
Eitan feels faint.

This shouldn't happen to boys who adore Arsenal, who buzz off quadratic equations, who pray to HaShem, who go camping with Zionist Youth movements and whose parents are happily married… God you mysterious fucker! Sort me out!

AVI *gets out of the Mikvah.*

EITAN *gets out of the Mikvah.*

*They dry themselves.*

AVI. Don't worry about it. I used to get them in geography lessons. Teacher would be talking about nimbus clouds and… whoop.

EITAN. You're married.

AVI. Yeah, you know Leyla, don't you?

EITAN. I think so.

AVI. At synagogue she sits up on the left, quite near your mum.

EITAN. Dark hair and green eyes?

AVI. Exactly.

EITAN. All the men look at her. She's piff. You're lucky, you're lucky to have married someone piff. Also she's dark, I like dark… like she almost looks Ethiopian, is she a convert?

AVI. No.

EITAN. You happily married?

AVI. Yes.

EITAN. My parents are happily married.

AVI. Okay. That's good to hear.

EITAN. How old were you when you got married?

AVI. Twenty-seven.

EITAN. Twenty-seven. Good age.

AVI. Well you can't plan these things.

EITAN. You can try.

AVI. You don't need to try.

EITAN. I could get a wife one day.

AVI. You could – you will.

EITAN. I can't breathe.

AVI. Whoa what do you mean

EITAN. I'm finding it hard to breathe

AVI. Relax, um, shit, do you need a doctor!?


EITAN *lies on the floor.*

EITAN. I'll be fine.


EITAN *gets up.*

AVI. Has this happened before?

EITAN. No

I want to fall in love.

AVI. It'll happen.

EITAN. When?

AVI. Soon.

EITAN. How will I know?

AVI. It is impossible to know. There is fun in the surprise. But one day you'll meet someone.

EITAN. And then what.

AVI. Er… she'll listen to your anxieties and laugh at your bad jokes.

EITAN. Sounds proper romantic. Baruch HaShem we have Hollywood.

AVI. Look it's less passionate than Hollywood but more
    constant. It hums underneath everything and then sort of
    pricks you awake.
    A best friend that morphs into a lover that morphs into a
    slave, a master and then morphs back into a best friend. Or
    all of those things together, at once, fluid, and then silence.
    All types of silence. Some comfortable, others savage.
    Shared silence on holidays, car journeys, in restaurants. And
    cruelty, there will be some cruelty, but if it's an honest
    marriage, there will always be…
    Cuddles.

EITAN. Alright Walt Disney.

AVI. We're in a Mikvah, you get my drift.

EITAN. Can't see myself on holiday in a restaurant or sharing a
    silence. I can't see any of that.

AVI. Well you're seventeen, I couldn't either.

EITAN. I bet you could.

AVI. It doesn't matter, it will happen.

EITAN. Shall we have a pint?

AVI. What?

EITAN. What?

AVI. I'll see you in shul tomorrow.

**Scene Six**

EITAN. Tomorrow.

AVI. We're in synagogue for Shabbat. Pausing life's noise.

EITAN. Yawn.

AVI. The service finishes.

EITAN. That's a relief. I'm starving.
Leave the synagogue, run to the hall, on the entrance two old
ladies hand out wine, whisky, whine, whisky, wine, I'll take
the tray, eh you can't do that, I've just done it, move across
the hall, It's Ben Hymi's bar mitzvah so we got tables piled
high with burekas, bagels, latkes, hummus, fish balls, fruit –
I get involved, then find a corner.

AVI. The hall is packed with people shaking hands, kissing and
hugging, everybody is fighting to get near the food table

EITAN. I've had four whiskies and six glasses of wine

AVI. It's a comfort to be touched on the arm, to whisper a joke,
to gossip.

EITAN. Little cups but still.

AVI. A sweet old woman winks at me.

EITAN. Avi's talking to that wrinkly inbred Mrs Menachem.

AVI. 'Nu, when are you going to be a papa?' she says.

EITAN. Creep up behind him slowly.
Brush his bum, gentle

AVI. 'Mrs Menachem, don't worry – soon – no rush – we're
making plans.'

EITAN. Then I walk to the end of the hall.

AVI. 'If you want to make God laugh – make plans.'

EITAN. Heart is beating.
   I'm pumped up!

AVI. Where's Leyla!?

EITAN. Maybe he didn't notice.

AVI. There she is.

EITAN. Eat some sushi. Fuck – this kiddush is amazing!

AVI. Laughing.
   Now deep in thought.

EITAN. He must not have felt my hand.
   Go in for a second

AVI. How does she do that?

   EITAN *walks across the hall and brushes* AVI's *bottom.*

   Shabbat Shalom.

EITAN. Shabbat Shalom.

AVI. Hows school?

EITAN. Yeah.

AVI. Have you got a girlfriend?

## Scene Seven

EITAN. It's science on a Monday. Eitan is looking at Rachel.
   She's rolled up her skirt so it looks like a belt.
   Rachel is always being told off by the Jewish studies
   teachers for rolling up her skirt.
   Mr Lobotinez is a perv though, so Rachel's all belt today.
   Eitan lies his head on the desk and looks underneath his arm
   to see up Rachel's skirt.

Her knickers are white.

Catch me looking. She doesn't. No one does.

Now Rachel is taking off her jumper. Every single person in the room notices this. The jumper catches on her shirt and we all glimpse her purple bra.

Rachel has really big boobs. I imagine the boobs as hot-air balloons lifting her up into the sky.

There she is floating. Hello Rachel.

Then the balloons pop and she plummets down to earth, dying on impact.

### Scene Eight

AVI *starts to undress*.

EITAN *starts to undress*.

AVI. Do you have a sport? Footy?

EITAN. Table tennis.

AVI. Okay.

EITAN. It's a great game. It also perfect for playing against yourself.

AVI. How does that work?

EITAN. I put up half the table. Just hit it back to myself.

AVI. Right. You ever played golf?

EITAN. Nah, saving that for when I'm a granddad.

EITAN *gets into the Mikvah*.

AVI. Ah. I find it helps me work things out. You should try it?

AVI *gets into the Mikvah*.

EITAN *and* AVI *immerse*.

EITAN *kisses* AVI. AVI *pushes* EITAN *under the water.*

AVI *leaves the Mikvah*.

What happened there mate?

EITAN. Eitan wonders why Avi called him 'mate'.

AVI. Well?

EITAN. The blood is racing between my heart and head.

AVI. Say something!?

EITAN. Eitan, stop thinking in the third person, talk to him
    Come in the Mikvah

AVI. No!

EITAN. The water feels particularly holy today.

AVI. Do you want to explain what just happened mate?

EITAN. Nothing happened.

AVI. Okay.
    Good.
    Let's just forget about it.

EITAN. I don't know if I can do that.

AVI. What!?

    Young people are always going through phases.

EITAN. Phases!?

AVI. I used to be obsessed with Warhammer.

EITAN. Oh yeah, what did ya collect?

AVI. Elves.

EITAN. I'm Ultramarines.

AVI. You're into Warhammer!?

EITAN. The games are shit but I like to paint the figurines.

AVI. My point is that I'm no longer into Warhammer.

EITAN. Lucky you. I reckon I'm gonna be painting Ultramarines for life.

AVI. Don't be ridiculous. Just choose not to paint Ultramarines.

EITAN. You're chatting breeze bruv.

AVI. Perhaps you could speak to a therapist...?

EITAN. What are you on about?

AVI. Have you ever felt so mad you could kill someone?

EITAN. Yeah.

AVI. But you don't right. You don't kill that person. You're not an animal, you're human, you have choices, you can choose to override your...

EITAN. So can you.

AVI. What?

Football fans occasionally waver don't they –

EITAN. Do you want to stop talking?

AVI. So let's say you're a Spurs fan.

EITAN. I'm a Gunner.

AVI. Okay so you're a Gunner, an Arsenal fan since forever right, but there might be a moment in your life where that Gunner has a desire, an urge, a flash of madness where he supports Spurs, but as quick as that moment arrives, it then evaporates and he forgets his Spurs moment ever happened and he returns to wholeheartedly supporting Arsenal.

EITAN. That is the lamest thing I've ever heard in my life.

AVI. Are you...?

EITAN. Of course I'm not.
But when we talk there's a, it feels like... we get each other.

AVI. Do kids bully you?

EITAN. What?

AVI. It's a simple question. Are you bullied?

EITAN. Why you suddenly asking this?

AVI. I bet they do. There's something so wimpy about you.

*Beat.*

That was inexcusable.

EITAN. It's cool, cool

AVI. It's not, it's not cool.

EITAN. Chill mofo.

AVI. There is nothing wimpy about you.

EITAN. Don't be such a pussy 'ole.

AVI. Why do Jewish boys from Finchley speak like they're from Jamaica?

EITAN. Eitan looks down at his wrinkled skin.

AVI. Avi's feet root to the spot.

## Scene Nine

AVI. It's Friday night.
    I sit opposite Leyla at the dinner table.
    She is talking in an animated way.
    There are specks of coriander in her teeth.
    The talk inevitably leads to 'children'. All roads lead to a baby.
    I imagine us as pandas. And the whole world gawking.
    I remember what happened in the Mikvah.
    The boy. The kiss.
    My chest tightens. I'm sweating.
    Leyla, I'm just going out for some air.
    She says 'Okay, do you want coffee?'
    Outside I'm trying to breathe.
    The sound of the kitchen clock is deafening.

Images of him invade…

EITAN. Avi collapses on the patio.
Leyla doesn't hear the thud.

We're in the woods.
It's freezing but we're having a laugh just you and me
Look at the trees.
The branches have been cut to stubs.
They look like amputees.
We climb up the trunk and sit ourselves on one of the stubs.
There is enough space for two.
This is a viiiiibe.
Get the thermos out!

AVI. Leyla shall we

EITAN. Feels like we've got our own special place.

AVI. Let's go away.

EITAN. Look at my breath, the steam

AVI. To be together.

EITAN. Oy, I forgot to tell you, I'm a dragon.

AVI. Just you and me.

EITAN. I said I'm a dragon.

AVI. Let's book a

EITAN. Like I breathe fire and shit.

AVI. Hotel

EITAN. Look at me

AVI. Leyla –

EITAN. I burn you. Actual fire comes out. Flames dance across
your body. Your skin starts to fry and peel off and then
everything shrinks and leaks, and yet, despite this rather
unfortunate situation, you're looking at me, like wanting me,
like ON IT.

AVI. Avi opens his eyes.
   The patio is wet.
   Blinks. Focuses.
   Alive.


## Scene Ten

AVI. Hey Leyla.
   Should we adopt?
   A child.
   Because I love you and we will be wonderful parents.

EITAN. I am not adopting a child. We are not adopting a child.

AVI. She isn't saying this.

EITAN. Yes she is.

AVI. Leyla.
   She says I don't want another person's genes in our child.
   I've married Doctor Mengele.
   She says You won't see any of us in our child.
   And what is so wrong with that?
   I don't recognise you.
   I'm still here.
   Are you?
   Yes.
   I don't want to adopt. I have no real reason as to why.
   So?
   Be patient my love, have faith.

   AVI *throws himself into a wall.*

**Scene Eleven**

EITAN. You're bleeding.

AVI. Am I?
　Oh.
　Shouldn't be in the Mikvah with blood.

EITAN. You want a plaster?

AVI. Yeah

EITAN. I got one in my bag. But maybe wash the cut first?

AVI. …

> AVI *looks at* EITAN.

EITAN. I got Nurofen and paracetemol if you're in pain, are
　you in pain?

AVI. No.

EITAN. My mum kitted out my school bag like a mobile
　pharmacy. Holla if you need anything.

AVI. Jewish mothers eh?

EITAN. Not really – she's a terrible cook.

AVI. Why do you come to the Mikvah?

EITAN. … to be spiritually cleansed.

AVI. That's not really the truth is it. I mean I'm sure it's part of
　the truth, but that's not the underlying reason, is it?

EITAN. I guess.

AVI. I think it's closer to why a convert immerses in the
　Mikvah.
　You know, rebirth.

EITAN. Maybe

AVI. Yes.

EITAN. Not sure that's the reason any more.

*Beat.*

AVI. I immerse in the Mikvah, so my sperm will… swim.
We want a child.

EITAN. You must have failed biology.

AVI. Yes.
When you love someone, I love her from my core, you are
willing to do anything.

EITAN. I get that.

AVI. Now. Here. I meet you. Some would suspect this, this
friendship as… I don't know.
Dangerous

EITAN. What's the danger?
I'm almost certain I could take you.

AVI. Perhaps if you drugged me.

EITAN. I'm down for that.

AVI *and* EITAN *laugh.*

AVI. Keep the sperm-swimming thing to yourself.
I love Leyla.

EITAN. Ease up bruv. You want to be a dad so you're taking
matters into your own hands. And it's not like you're praying
for something material, like a Porsche. So let's hope
HaShem is listening. I think you'd be a jokes dad.

AVI. Thank you.

EITAN. I want to touch you – I won't – But I want to.
Sorry.

AVI. Imagine.

EITAN. What?

AVI. Imagine… touching…

EITAN. I'd like to…

AVI. …

EITAN. I'm touching

AVI. …

EITAN. Your back

AVI. …

EITAN. It's warm

AVI. …

EITAN. Firm.

AVI. …

EITAN. My hand runs down it.

AVI. …

EITAN. I'm stroking

AVI. …

EITAN. Your thigh

AVI. Your hand

EITAN. Skin

AVI. On

EITAN. Now we're…

AVI. Stop.

## ACT TWO

### Scene One

AVI. Avi runs to John Lewis and buys a record player.
Then realises he doesn't own any records.
So he runs to a second-hand music shop.
He buys Fatboy Slim, a flashback to his youth, when he
should of gone to clubs, but didn't, Marvin Gaye's *Piece of
Clay* oh and Barbra Streisand! For a laugh!
He rushes home and throws the present at Leyla.
It catches her off-guard. It's not her birthday or anything.
'We've got four minutes till Shabbat, so time for one song'
Plug in the record player.

*Music.*

AVI *dances 'Leyla' around the room.*

The song finishes and I hold her because I never want to let
her go.
We make love.
It's different this time.

### Scene Two

EITAN. I'm waiting in the café. I'm sipping on a large hot
chocolate.
Stupid drink, childish.
Legs twitch palms clam. Breathe.

AVI. Avi walks into the café.

EITAN. Good shirt.

AVI. Eitan looks wired, oh God he's not on drugs is he?

EITAN. I'm fantasising about digging my nails into his chest.

AVI. Thanks for meeting me here at relatively short notice.

EITAN. It's all good bossman, managed to find a bit of free time, you know how it is, busy at this time of year isn't it?

AVI. Is it?

So the reason I invited you here...

EITAN. Spill the beans, let the cat out, give the game away.

AVI. The reason is... to explain that after this meeting we must have no further contact. Of course we will see each other in synagogue, but I prefer it if you didn't approach me. I have found another Mikvah further away so there will be no possibility of us bumping into each other, if you stick to your Mikvah and I stick to mine.

EITAN. Yeah I'm not really down for that.

So you know how I got three thousand, four hundred and twenty pounds for my bar mitzvah?

AVI. ...

EITAN. Well a lot of people at school blew their bar mitzvah money on dumb shit like PlayStations or noble shit like adopting an Israeli orphan.

AVI. You can't just adopt an Israeli orphan.

EITAN. Whatever.
I've booked us a weekend away in Alicante.
Four-star hotel, two minutes from the beach.
Are you on it?

AVI. Sure. Can't wait.

EITAN. Quality!!! I thought I'd have to take you hostage to get you there.

AVI. What are you talking about?

EITAN. An all-inclusive package.

AVI. Are you mad?

EITAN. They've got a golf course, you could teach me.

AVI. I'm not gonna go away with you.

EITAN. Why not?

AVI. What!? A thirty-five-year-old man does not go on holiday
with a boy

EITAN. Why not?

AVI. ... I'm married.

EITAN. You like me otherwise you wouldn't have let me
imagine

AVI. The little imaginary game in the Mikvah didn't mean
anything.

EITAN. I don't believe you.

AVI. What don't you believe?

EITAN. I don't believe a word you say.

AVI. I want to destroy you.

EITAN (*smiling*). Okay.

   AVI *tries to exit*.

   Please wait, please, look, what if we lived on the moon

AVI. What!?

EITAN. No. Wait. Not the moon. If we were reborn, not as
Jews, just as I dunno, people, no particular religion, just
British people, who don't believe in God or anything. So
we're born and we grow up, and we don't know each other
or anything, but one day we're on a beach, in, in the
Maldives, and we're in the sea, and we just start chatting and
we get on really well, like it's astonishing how we just click
as if we have known each other our whole lives, and we're
having jokes, and I'm not seventeen I'm twenty-seven, but

you're still thirty-five and, you're single, so not married, and I say fancy, fancy coming to have a burger, or cos it's the Maldives, it would be more like a fish curry, so would you fancy having a fish curry...?

AVI. Yes. As a friend.

EITAN. Well come to Alicante as a friend.

AVI. I can't.

EITAN. But I'll have a brilliant tan.

AVI. Eitan, I'm married to Leyla.

EITAN. I'll kill her

AVI. What?

EITHAN. Maybe you can love two people at the same time?

AVI. I don't.

EITAN. How do you know?

AVI. Thinking about you makes me nauseous.

EITAN. Wow. I've never had that effect on anybody.

AVI. Oh don't do that,

EITAN. I'm not crying.

AVI. This will blow over next week you won't remember

EITAN. Please stop fucking lying

AVI. Okay.

EITAN. I'm crying.

> [*Italic text changes according to daily football news. Actors should decide on incident before each performance. Below is an example.*]

AVI. *What do you make of Danny Welbeck?*

EITAN. *Worth sixteen mill.*

AVI. *Not exactly clinical in front of goal though is he?*

EITAN. *He's got four so far, give him a chance – wait –*

Who are you again?

AVI. Tottenham mate.

EITAN. Yer fucking not?
(*Almost laughs.*)
A Yid.
Typical.

What happens now?

AVI. We walk out of the café.

EITAN. Is this the last time we speak?

AVI. Yes.

EITAN. Not the end of the world – I was always more into your lips than your chat.

AVI. Well you can't have either.

EITAN. Who am I gonna take to Alicante?

AVI. Your mother

EITAN. I'll take a mate.

AVI. You don't have any.

EITAN. It'll have to be a male escort, then.

AVI. That'll be alright – you've got your bar mitzvah money.

EITAN. Are you for hire?

AVI. You can't afford me.

EITAN. I can pay two thousand, nine hundred and twenty-eight pounds.

AVI. I'm scared of flying.

EITAN. Sod Ryanair then, we'll coach it to Alicante.

AVI. Do you always have an answer?

EITAN. Wagwan, allow we dust to the beach.

AVI. Stop speaking like you're black – you're not black

EITAN. If I'm raped abroad, it'll be on your conscience.

AVI. So be it.

EITAN. We both know you're coming.

AVI. What do I tell Leyla?

EITAN. I dunno, make something up. Married people lie all the time.

### Scene Three

AVI. We get a taxi from the airport to the hotel

*AVI and EITAN put on swimming costumes. They apply sun cream.*

*They jump in the pool – (the Mikvah).*

*Pool madness. Handstands, synchronised swimming, dunking.*

EITAN. Walk towards me like Daniel Craig

*AVI does his 'Daniel Craig' impression.*

AVI. You don't see me looking at you.

EITAN. You think I don't see you looking at me.

*AVI and EITAN get out of the water and go on a night out.*

*Holiday drinking and dancing – everything is wild and intoxicating.*

*Now they are opposite ends of the space, taking each other in.*

*Twilight.*

*They explore each other.*

## ACT THREE

### Scene One

AVI. I return home.
Leyla looks at me and begins to cry.
Oh no, she knows – what does she know!?
That's not why she's crying.
These are happy tears.
She mouths the words.
And now she's hugging me, she's squeezing the life out of me.
'We did it' she whispers over and over again.

EITAN. Damn Mikvah worked for you!

AVI. She moves my hand and places it on her stomach.

EITAN. That's cheesy, does she actually do that?

AVI. I pray the Mikvah works for you.

EITAN. Fuck off with your prayers.

AVI. Leyla, what can I do? What do you want? Get me yogurt-coated bananas from Holland and Barrett she says. Clear the shop she says. Yogurt-coated bananas! Unbelievable!

EITAN. Come on let's do a piggy back

AVI. Eitan, I'm gonna be a dad!


EITAN. Vroom, vroom, I'm driving, vroom vroom up the A41, in a Vauxhall Corsa, vroom, got mad tunes on – (*Beatboxes/sings a tune or beat.*) vroom, turn onto the M1, vroom, there it is – the Welcome Break – turn off, park the car, go to Starbucks, order a mocha, cor I'm buzzing, are we gonna do it in your car or mine?

We're on the thirty-second floor of the Shard, I can see the whole of London. We're in the restaurant bit. The gnocchi is exquisite.

We're deep-sea diving in the Galapagos Islands. Check out that squid thing hoovering up the seabed. It looks like Mrs Menachem.

We're in the cunting synagogue.

I'm in the Mikvah. You're here too. Please.

AVI *exits the stage*.

Hey.
Hey you.
I've left Leyla.
Wow.
I've moved into a one-bed flat, in… Shoreditch.
This set of keys is for you.

## Scene Two

AVI. It's Yom Kippur, the day of Atonement. Everyone is fasting.
Avi hasn't drunk or eaten in twenty-three hours.
The shul stinks of stale breath.
Is Eitan here?
Focus.
Focus on atoning.

AVI *lightly pounds his chest forty times, each time muttering a sin*.

EITAN. Eitan has yet to come to synagogue for the holiest day of the year. The absence is marked by his family, his community and Avi.
Still in possession of his brother's ID, Eitan whiles away the afternoon at the bookies. He slots coins into the fruit

machine and as he's hypnotized by the moving bananas and grapes and monkeys,

he thinks of the garden of Eden.

Buried deep in his mind a story...

When Adam was banished from Eden he sat in the river that flowed from the garden. That river was the very first Mikvah. Adam immersed in the water, praying, begging to return to an original state of perfection.

AVI *sings 'Avino Malcheinu'.*

The hairs on the back of my neck stand on end. My mother glares at me from the women's gallery – 'Where have you been?' My little brother is on the choir. My elder brother rocks back and forth like a mentalist. My dad is snoozing – his shirt bursting at the buttons as his tummy spills out. Eitan walks towards the bimah.

AVI *climbs the stairs.*

I stand next to him. Our shoulders touch. We breathe in and out at exactly the same time.

I miss you.

AVI *stops singing.*

AVI. Eitan

EITAN. Three hundred eyes bear down on us

AVI. Please.

EITAN. Avi is terrified.

AVI. Sit down.

EITAN. Avi

AVI. I'm begging you.

EITAN *leaves.*

AVI *resumes singing 'Avino Malcheino'.*

EITAN. I run to the Mikvah. Of course it's locked.
I take a brick – can't believe I'm doing this...

I throw the brick through the window.
I climb up and in
The alarm goes.
No matter.

EITAN *walks into the Mikvah fully clothed and tries to*
*drown himself.*

## Scene Three

AVI. Avi eats a tiny slice of a banana loaf.
    Leyla's not fasting this year on account of… our baby!
    How are you sweetheart?
    It feels odd to not have fasted.
    Enjoy the feeling. Next year you'll be back to stomach
    cramps and a migraine.
    Don't be dramatic.
    You weren't standing on the bimah all day.
    I'd happily have stood on the bimah all day.
    Oh yeah
    Anyway. Drink your tea, you'll be dehydrated.

Avi eats the entire loaf.

It's been twenty-five hours!
That boy Eitan walked up on the bimah today midway
through 'Avino Malcheino'.
Bit strange wasn't it?
Yeah.
He said something to you.
He's a weird kid.
What did he say?
He's got a crush on you hasn't he darling?
Don't be stupid
Poor boy, what a nightmare his life is gonna be.
The doorbell rings.

EITAN *enters.*

EITAN. Leyla says hello.

She says 'You're soaking.'

She says 'We didn't hear the rain did we, darling?'

AVI. It isn't raining.

EITAN. Leyla invites me in.

AVI. What?

EITAN. She says 'Av go and get some of warm clothes
otherwise Eitan will catch pneumonia.'

AVI *leaves*.

How did you fast?
I didn't either
I tell Leyla I don't believe in HaShem so it would be
pointless to fast.
I tell her I know she's pregnant.
I tell her she's beautiful, perfect.
Then I kiss her, to see what she tastes of.

Avi arrives with clothes.

AVI. Eitan leaves.

Why did Eitan come over.
I don't know
He just kissed me.
Did he?

Av what's going on?
I unburden myself
Eitan and I we had a moment, it was a strange sort of thing
that just happened and I can't explain why but I went away
with him, I lied about the golf trip, I mean I did play golf but
it was with Eitan. I thought I could change him and we got
on so well and he looked up to me but then things got very
confused… and we kissed.
Leyla gasps
It will never happen again
Leyla still doesn't breathe

She says you went away with a seventeen-year-old boy?
Yes.
She says you kissed a seventeen-year-old boy?
Yes.
Are you...?
No, no, no, no
Do you love him?
I love you!! It got mixed up, me trying to be a – he'd come
to the Mikvah, and he was very alone, it is very, it was
undefined and fucked, I don't want anyone else but you.
This is so exhilarating to share, to speak it all out loud to
somebody, and although it damages, it is so good to release
The room is still.
Leyla's voice is hoarse.
And it's over?
Yes.
Leyla is numb.
The boy was a test sent from HaShem. He was a test.
The room is still.
Leyla pulls me towards her
Then drags us down onto the floor.

**Scene Four**

EITAN. I could ruin you.

AVI. I've told Leyla.

EITAN. What about my mum, my dad, brothers, Rabbi Ovadiah –

AVI. They don't need to know.

EITAN. Why?

AVI. Because we have something they won't understand.

EITAN. That's a line you say to a child to keep them quiet.
    I'm not a child.

AVI. Tell them then.
   If that's what you want.

EITAN. D'ya think once you have the baby, the ache, will just
   disappear?

AVI. I don't know.

EITAN. You're going to walk away from this!?

AVI. There is no 'this'. It was a moment.

EITAN. The water. The beach. The hotel room. Those
   experiences are tattooed on our bodies.

AVI. I'm sorry.

EITAN. And the Mikvah!? Every time you immerse I am here.

AVI. It must hurt.

EITAN. You can't look at me.

AVI. I can.

EITAN. That's why you've spent so much time looking out.

AVI. I'm looking at you now.

EITAN. And what do you see?

AVI. A young man. A friend.

EITAN. A friend!?

AVI. Nothing more.

EITAN. You're fucking delusional. We're in love.

   EITAN *tries to kiss* AVI. *They wrestle.*

   AVI *puts his hand in the Mikvah waters.*

   You're still looking out.

AVI. This will get easier.

EITAN. That doesn't help me now.

AVI. One week passes. How do you feel?

EITAN. Like I've lost an arm.

AVI. Two months pass

EITAN. Feel ghostly, detached, not here, not anywhere.

AVI. Four months pass.

EITAN. I prank-call you like thirteen times.

AVI. Seven months pass.

EITAN. I cry once in the swimming-pool showers.

AVI. Nine months pass. Do you feel any better?

EITAN. If you mean not suicidal…?

AVI. I have a son.

EITAN. Mazel tov!

AVI. Today is the brit milah.

EITAN. I tend to vomit at circumcisions.

AVI. Is it the utensils?

EITAN. Or faint.

AVI. The mohel gets out cotton wool, a suction device, a knife, baby wipes

EITAN. Shut up.

AVI. He makes the cut. There's blood. My son lets out a sound, I've never heard before. I cradle him –

EITAN. Why are you telling us about the circumcision!?

AVI. Because despite the blood and that sound, I want this.
I want Leyla, my tiny boy, and the singing in shul.
At whatever cost.

EITAN. I see.
Perhaps I can cleanse myself of you?

AVI. Perhaps.

EITAN. That was a joke.

AVI. God ought to have given us the capacity to erase.

EITAN. Should I knock you out and we pray for amnesia?

AVI. Or
Maybe try drowning yourself again.

EITAN. How does that help you?

AVI. If you're not here, you're not here.

Now what.

EITAN. We try and part.

AVI. Very funny.

EITAN. No seriously.
Let us try and part.
I'm ready.

AVI. Is this what you want?

EITAN. I'm a bit nervous.

*The End.*

**A Nick Hern Book**

*Buggy Baby & The Mikvah Project* first published in Great Britain in 2018 as a paperback original by Nick Hern Books Limited, The Glasshouse, 49a Goldhawk Road, London W12 8QP, in association with The Yard, London

*Buggy Baby & The Mikvah Project* copyright © 2018 Josh Azouz

Josh Azouz has asserted his moral right to be identified as the author of these works

Cover image: Heather Perkins

Designed and typeset by Nick Hern Books, London
Printed in the UK by Mimeo Ltd, Huntingdon, Cambridgeshire PE29 6XX

A CIP catalogue record for this book is available from the British Library

ISBN 978 1 84842 747 1

Woodland
CARBON
www.woodlandcarbon.co.uk
NICK HERN BOOKS
Printed on Carbon Captured paper